5S Office Evaluation Review

Date: _____   Evaluation Area: _____

5S Element	Number	Evaluation Criteria	Rank these items from 1 through 5: 5 being well done	Score (1-5)	Ideas / Suggestions / Comments
SORT	I	Are the aisles and walkways open and clear?	All items that are not necessary or unsafe have been removed from the area used as pathways.		
	II	Is the office area free of any spills of fluids?	Consider whether there are any chemicals, water, oils or other materials that may be hazardous in the area or on the floor.		
	III	Is the office area free of unnecessary articles and items?	Are items that are not needed been removed from the work zone, i.e. monitors, scanners, stationary, extra items?		
	IV	Is the office area free of excess consumables/materials?	Evaluate against how many items are in the processing area for work. Assess if the materials, parts, and supplies in the area are currently needed for the job. Closer to actually needed is better.		
	V	Is the information board active?	All announcements are displayed currently and in good presentable shape. Arrangement is straight and placed under appropriate headings.		
	VI	Are the areas walls and dividers free of items not used in the operation?	Extra items are not on the walls, dividers, calendars, or hanging of posters that are not necessary.		
			Category Subtotal		
			Sort Score: Subtotal divided by 6		
SET IN ORDER / STRAIGHTEN	VII	Evaluate any documentation storage.	Only documents required for jobs are stored at the point of use. These documents are stored nicely and in an orderly fashion that is recognizable/understandable to outsiders.		
	VIII	How are the shelves, desks, and work surfaces arranged?	All locations of items are labeled, marked, and it is known if they are missing.		
	IX	How are the tools and materials stored in the area?	No items are resting on walls, tucked in corners. No items are resting on equipment, cupboards, or other fixtures.		
	X	Evaluate container and any packaging locations and tidiness.	Boxes, storage containers, and other items are stored in the appropriate place and orientated well for the area. Cabinets are secure and not causing any danger to the people working in the area.		
	XI	Assess order and where items are found on the floor.	Nothing is sitting directly on the floor and no materials are left around the area. Items that need to be on the floor are clearly marked and positioned in designated areas clearly outlined on the floor.		
	XII	Easiness to access the tools, equipment, and stationary.	Materials, tools, jigs, attachments, and fixtures are organized so that they are all easily within reach. Consider this as well for any kind of tools needed for a job including cutting and measuring something.		
			Category Subtotal		
			Set in Order / Straighten Score: Subtotal divided by 6		
SHINE / SWEEP	XIII	The storage of templates and any tools.	Arrangement of all templates, tools, and materials are kept in clean area for storage and no risk of losing information during movements around office.		
	XIV	Clear when equipment needs maintenance and when last maintained.	Instructions on equipment in the office is marked, highlighted, and labeled. Check sheets available for high value equipment. Maintenance is scheduled for critical equipment.		
	XV	Assess the cleanliness of the office.	How dust free are the areas? This may be critical. Look under desks and behind work spaces to see if there is garbage and other unnecessary items.		
	XVI	Assess status of equipment in the area. Cleanliness overall appearance.	Are machines and equipment known to be on a schedule of cleaning?		
			Category Subtotal		
			Shine / Sweep Score: Subtotal divided by 4		
STANDARDIZE	XVII	Is there visual color diagramming and color coding?	A clear and present color coding system is present in the office and across departments. It is clear that standards are being maintained and improved on.		
	XVIII	Assess the access ways in case of emergency.	All emergency systems; fire vehicles, fire extinguishers, and emergency equipment free of obstruction and clear at all times. Access to electrical controls and fuses are known, marked, and free of any obstructions.		
	XIX	The aisle ways are bright with light and clearly marked.	Walkways are clearly highlighted for direction, aisle access identified at any moment.		
	XX	General area has quantity limits for materials and are marked clearly.	Heights are marked, quantity of materials are known, and min vs. max. This includes paper for machines, number of computers required, toner levels, graphical paper, and special office material needed.		
	XXI	Is there clear document control of information in the office?	All information and documentation is controlled, labeled, and revisions are up to date. There are no label-less binders or pieces of paper in the area.		
			Category Subtotal		
			Standardize Score: Subtotal divided by 5		
SUSTAIN	XXII	The aisle ways are clean and maintenance is clear.	Aisles are never full of anything and are clear for passage. All items and products not stored in the aisle and storage is next to aisle accessible for transportation.		
	XXIII	Illustrations and office layout plans are available to compare against.	5S has a maintenance system that allows for control of change and improvement of 5S in the office. Scoring is kept on each of these items and history is present and visible to support future improvement.		
	XXIV	Ability for shared resources and tools to be set back in place for storage.	No self-discipline is necessary to ensure that all stationary, tools, templates, materials, and shared equipment is put back in the same spot. The effort of putting back should not require organizational skills.		
	XXV	Evaluate the involvement of managers in 5S.	Managers are actively involved in the review process of 5S and are supporting improvement activities of the office.		
			Category Subtotal		
			Sustain Score: Subtotal divided by 4		**Total "Category Subtotals" divide by 25 average 5 S score: TOTAL**

5S Office Evaluation Review

Date: _____   Evaluation Area: _____

5S Element	Number	Evaluation Criteria	Rank these items from 1 through 5: 5 being well done	Score (1-5)	Ideas / Suggestions / Comments
SORT	I	Are the aisles and walkways open and clear?	All items that are not necessary or unsafe have been removed from the area used as pathways.		
	II	Is the office area free of any spills of fluids?	Consider whether there are any chemicals, water, oils or other materials that may be hazardous in the area or on the floor.		
	III	Is the office area free of unnecessary articles and items?	Are items that are not needed been removed from the work zone, i.e. monitors, scanners, stationary, extra items?		
	IV	Is the office area free of excess consumables/materials?	Evaluate against how many items are in the processing area for work. Assess if the materials, parts, and supplies in the area are currently needed for the job. Closer to actually needed is better.		
	V	Is the information board active?	All announcements are displayed currently and in good presentable shape. Arrangement is straight and placed under appropriate headings.		
	VI	Are the areas walls and dividers free of items not used in the operation?	Extra items are not on the walls, dividers, calendars, or hanging of posters that are not necessary.		
		Category Subtotal			
		Sort Score: Subtotal divided by 6			
SET IN ORDER / STRAIGHTEN	VII	Evaluate any documentation storage.	Only documents required for jobs are stored at the point of use. These documents are stored nicely and in an orderly fashion that is recognizable/understandable to outsiders.		
	VIII	How are the shelves, desks, and work surfaces arranged?	All locations of items are labeled, marked, and it is known if they are missing.		
	IX	How are the tools and materials stored in the area?	No items are resting on walls, tucked in corners. No items are resting on equipment, cupboards, or other fixtures.		
	X	Evaluate container and any packaging locations and tidiness.	Boxes, storage containers, and other items are stored in the appropriate place and orientated well for the area. Cabinets are secure and not causing any danger to the people working in the area.		
	XI	Assess order and where items are found on the floor.	Nothing is sitting directly on the floor and no materials are left around the area. Items that need to be on the floor are clearly marked and positioned in designated areas clearly outlined on the floor.		
	XII	Easiness to access the tools, equipment, and stationary.	Materials, tools, jigs, attachments, and fixtures are organized so that they are all easily within reach. Consider this as well for any kind of tools needed for a job including cutting and measuring something.		
		Category Subtotal			
		Set in Order / Straighten Score: Subtotal divided by 6			
SHINE / SWEEP	XIII	The storage of templates and any tools.	Arrangement of all templates, tools, and materials are kept in clean area for storage and no risk of losing information during movements around office.		
	XIV	Clear when equipment needs maintenance and when last maintained.	Instructions on equipment in the office is marked, highlighted, and labeled. Check sheets available for high value equipment. Maintenance is scheduled for critical equipment.		
	XV	Assess the cleanliness of the office.	How dust free are the areas? This may be critical. Look under desks and behind work spaces to see if there is garbage and other unnecessary items.		
	XVI	Assess status of equipment in the area. Cleanliness overall appearance.	Are machines and equipment known to be on a schedule of cleaning?		
		Category Subtotal			
		Shine / Sweep Score: Subtotal divided by 4			
STANDARDIZE	XVII	Is there visual color diagramming and color coding?	A clear and present color coding system is present in the office and across departments. It is clear that standards are being maintained and improved on.		
	XVIII	Assess the access ways in case of emergency.	All emergency systems; fire vehicles, fire extinguishers, and emergency equipment free of obstruction and clear at all times. Access to electrical controls and fuses are known, marked, and free of any obstructions.		
	XIX	The aisle ways are bright with light and clearly marked.	Walkways are clearly highlighted for direction, aisle access identified at any moment.		
	XX	General area has quantity limits for materials and are marked clearly.	Heights are marked, quantity of materials are known, and min vs. max. This includes paper for machines, number of computers required, toner levels, graphical paper, and special office material needed.		
	XXI	Is there clear document control of information in the office?	All information and documentation is controlled, labeled, and revisions are up to date. There are no label-less binders or pieces of paper in the area.		
		Category Subtotal			
		Standardize Score: Subtotal divided by 5			
SUSTAIN	XXII	The aisle ways are clean and maintenance is clear.	Aisles are never full of anything and are clear for passage. All items and products not stored in the aisle and storage is next to aisle accessible for transportation.		
	XXIII	Illustrations and office layout plans are available to compare against.	5S has a maintenance system that allows for control of change and improvement of 5S in the office. Scoring is kept on each of these items and history is present and visible to support future improvement.		
	XXIV	Ability for shared resources and tools to be set back in place for storage.	No self-discipline is necessary to ensure that all stationary, tools, templates, materials, and shared equipment is put back in the same spot. The effort of putting back should not require organizational skills.		
	XXV	Evaluate the involvement of managers in 5S.	Managers are actively involved in the review process of 5S and are supporting improvement activities of the office.		
		Category Subtotal			
		Sustain Score: Subtotal divided by 4		**Total "Category Subtotals" divide by 25 average 5 S score: TOTAL**

5S Office Evaluation Review

Date: _____   Evaluation Area: _____

5S Element	Number	Evaluation Criteria	Rank these items from 1 through 5: 5 being well done	Score (1-5)	Ideas / Suggestions / Comments
SORT	I	Are the aisles and walkways open and clear?	All items that are not necessary or unsafe have been removed from the area used as pathways.		
	II	Is the office area free of any spills of fluids?	Consider whether there are any chemicals, water, oils or other materials that may be hazardous in the area or on the floor.		
	III	Is the office area free of unnecessary articles and items?	Are items that are not needed been removed from the work zone, i.e. monitors, scanners, stationary, extra items?		
	IV	Is the office area free of excess consumables/materials?	Evaluate against how many items are in the processing area for work. Assess if the materials, parts, and supplies in the area are currently needed for the job. Closer to actually needed is better.		
	V	Is the information board active?	All announcements are displayed currently and in good presentable shape. Arrangement is straight and placed under appropriate headings.		
	VI	Are the areas walls and dividers free of items not used in the operation?	Extra items are not on the walls, dividers, calendars, or hanging of posters that are not necessary.		
			Category Subtotal		
			Sort Score: Subtotal divided by 6		
SET IN ORDER / STRAIGHTEN	VII	Evaluate any documentation storage.	Only documents required for jobs are stored at the point of use. These documents are stored nicely and in an orderly fashion that is recognizable/understandable to outsiders.		
	VIII	How are the shelves, desks, and work surfaces arranged?	All locations of items are labeled, marked, and it is known if they are missing.		
	IX	How are the tools and materials stored in the area?	No items are resting on walls, tucked in corners. No items are resting on equipment, cupboards, or other fixtures.		
	X	Evaluate container and any packaging locations and tidiness.	Boxes, storage containers, and other items are stored in the appropriate place and orientated well for the area. Cabinets are secure and not causing any danger to the people working in the area.		
	XI	Assess order and where items are found on the floor.	Nothing is sitting directly on the floor and no materials are left around the area. Items that need to be on the floor are clearly marked and positioned in designated areas clearly outlined on the floor.		
	XII	Easiness to access the tools, equipment, and stationary.	Materials, tools, jigs, attachments, and fixtures are organized so that they are all easily within reach. Consider this as well for any kind of tools needed for a job including cutting and measuring something.		
			Category Subtotal		
			Set in Order / Straighten Score: Subtotal divided by 6		
SHINE / SWEEP	XIII	The storage of templates and any tools.	Arrangement of all templates, tools, and materials are kept in clean area for storage and no risk of losing information during movements around office.		
	XIV	Clear when equipment needs maintenance and when last maintained.	Instructions on equipment in the office is marked, highlighted, and labeled. Check sheets available for high value equipment. Maintenance is scheduled for critical equipment.		
	XV	Assess the cleanliness of the office.	How dust free are the areas? This may be critical. Look under desks and behind work spaces to see if there is garbage and other unnecessary items.		
	XVI	Assess status of equipment in the area. Cleanliness overall appearance.	Are machines and equipment known to be on a schedule of cleaning?		
			Category Subtotal		
			Shine / Sweep Score: Subtotal divided by 4		
STANDARDIZE	XVII	Is there visual color diagramming and color coding?	A clear and present color coding system is present in the office and across departments. It is clear that standards are being maintained and improved on.		
	XVIII	Assess the access ways in case of emergency.	All emergency systems; fire vehicles, fire extinguishers, and emergency equipment free of obstruction and clear at all times. Access to electrical controls and fuses are known, marked, and free of any obstructions.		
	XIX	The aisle ways are bright with light and clearly marked.	Walkways are clearly highlighted for direction, aisle access identified at any moment.		
	XX	General area has quantity limits for materials and are marked clearly.	Heights are marked, quantity of materials are known, and min vs. max. This includes paper for machines, number of computers required, toner levels, graphical paper, and special office material needed.		
	XXI	Is there clear document control of information in the office?	All information and documentation is controlled, labeled, and revisions are up to date. There are no label-less binders or pieces of paper in the area.		
			Category Subtotal		
			Standardize Score: Subtotal divided by 5		
SUSTAIN	XXII	The aisle ways are clean and maintenance is clear.	Aisles are never full of anything and are clear for passage. All items and products not stored in the aisle and storage is next to aisle accessible for transportation.		
	XXIII	Illustrations and office layout plans are available to compare against.	5S has a maintenance system that allows for control of change and improvement of 5S in the office. Scoring is kept on each of these items and history is present and visible to support future improvement.		
	XXIV	Ability for shared resources and tools to be set back in place for storage.	No self-discipline is necessary to ensure that all stationary, tools, templates, materials, and shared equipment is put back in the same spot. The effort of putting back should not require organizational skills.		
	XXV	Evaluate the involvement of managers in 5S.	Managers are actively involved in the review process of 5S and are supporting improvement activities of the office.		
			Category Subtotal		
			Sustain Score: Subtotal divided by 4		**Total "Category Subtotals" divide by 25 average 5 S score: TOTAL**

5S Office Evaluation Review

Date: _____   Evaluation Area: _____

5S Element	Number	Evaluation Criteria	Rank these items from 1 through 5: 5 being well done	Score (1-5)	Ideas / Suggestions / Comments
SORT	I	Are the aisles and walkways open and clear?	All items that are not necessary or unsafe have been removed from the area used as pathways.		
	II	Is the office area free of any spills of fluids?	Consider whether there are any chemicals, water, oils or other materials that may be hazardous in the area or on the floor.		
	III	Is the office area free of unnecessary articles and items?	Are items that are not needed been removed from the work zone, i.e. monitors, scanners, stationary, extra items?		
	IV	Is the office area free of excess consumables/materials?	Evaluate against how many items are in the processing area for work. Assess if the materials, parts, and supplies in the area are currently needed for the job. Closer to actually needed is better.		
	V	Is the information board active?	All announcements are displayed currently and in good presentable shape. Arrangement is straight and placed under appropriate headings.		
	VI	Are the areas walls and dividers free of items not used in the operation?	Extra items are not on the walls, dividers, calendars, or hanging of posters that are not necessary.		
			Category Subtotal	- - - - -	
			Sort Score: Subtotal divided by 6		
SET IN ORDER / STRAIGHTEN	VII	Evaluate any documentation storage.	Only documents required for jobs are stored at the point of use. These documents are stored nicely and in an orderly fashion that is recognizable/understandable to outsiders.		
	VIII	How are the shelves, desks, and work surfaces arranged?	All locations of items are labeled, marked, and it is known if they are missing.		
	IX	How are the tools and materials stored in the area?	No items are resting on walls, tucked in corners. No items are resting on equipment, cupboards, or other fixtures.		
	X	Evaluate container and any packaging locations and tidiness.	Boxes, storage containers, and other items are stored in the appropriate place and orientated well for the area. Cabinets are secure and not causing any danger to the people working in the area.		
	XI	Assess order and where items are found on the floor.	Nothing is sitting directly on the floor and no materials are left around the area. Items that need to be on the floor are clearly marked and positioned in designated areas clearly outlined on the floor.		
	XII	Easiness to access the tools, equipment, and stationary.	Materials, tools, jigs, attachments, and fixtures are organized so that they are all easily within reach. Consider this as well for any kind of tools needed for a job including cutting and measuring something.		
			Category Subtotal	- - - - -	
			Set in Order / Straighten Score: Subtotal divided by 6		
SHINE / SWEEP	XIII	The storage of templates and any tools.	Arrangement of all templates, tools, and materials are kept in clean area for storage and no risk of losing information during movements around office.		
	XIV	Clear when equipment needs maintenance and when last maintained.	Instructions on equipment in the office is marked, highlighted, and labeled. Check sheets available for high value equipment. Maintenance is scheduled for critical equipment.		
	XV	Assess the cleanliness of the office.	How dust free are the areas? This may be critical. Look under desks and behind work spaces to see if there is garbage and other unnecessary items.		
	XVI	Assess status of equipment in the area. Cleanliness overall appearance.	Are machines and equipment known to be on a schedule of cleaning?		
			Category Subtotal	- - - - -	
			Shine / Sweep Score: Subtotal divided by 4		
STANDARDIZE	XVII	Is there visual color diagramming and color coding?	A clear and present color coding system is present in the office and across departments. It is clear that standards are being maintained and improved on.		
	XVIII	Assess the access ways in case of emergency.	All emergency systems; fire vehicles, fire extinguishers, and emergency equipment free of obstruction and clear at all times. Access to electrical controls and fuses are known, marked, and free of any obstructions.		
	XIX	The aisle ways are bright with light and clearly marked.	Walkways are clearly highlighted for direction, aisle access identified at any moment.		
	XX	General area has quantity limits for materials and are marked clearly.	Heights are marked, quantity of materials are known, and min vs. max. This includes paper for machines, number of computers required, toner levels, graphical paper, and special office material needed.		
	XXI	Is there clear document control of information in the office?	All information and documentation is controlled, labeled, and revisions are up to date. There are no label-less binders or pieces of paper in the area.		
			Category Subtotal	- - - - -	
			Standardize Score: Subtotal divided by 5		
SUSTAIN	XXII	The aisle ways are clean and maintenance is clear.	Aisles are never full of anything and are clear for passage. All items and products not stored in the aisle and storage is next to aisle accessible for transportation.		
	XXIII	Illustrations and office layout plans are available to compare against.	5S has a maintenance system that allows for control of change and improvement of 5S in the office. Scoring is kept on each of these items and history is present and visible to support future improvement.		
	XXIV	Ability for shared resources and tools to be set back in place for storage.	No self-discipline is necessary to ensure that all stationary, tools, templates, materials, and shared equipment is put back in the same spot. The effort of putting back should not require organizational skills.		
	XXV	Evaluate the involvement of managers in 5S.	Managers are actively involved in the review process of 5S and are supporting improvement activities of the office.		
			Category Subtotal	- - - - -	
			Sustain Score: Subtotal divided by 4		**Total "Category Subtotals" divide by 25 average 5 S score: TOTAL**

5S Office Evaluation Review

Date: _____   Evaluation Area: _____

5S Element	Number	Evaluation Criteria	Rank these items from 1 through 5: 5 being well done	Score (1-5)	Ideas / Suggestions / Comments
SORT	I	Are the aisles and walkways open and clear?	All items that are not necessary or unsafe have been removed from the area used as pathways.		
	II	Is the office area free of any spills of fluids?	Consider whether there are any chemicals, water, oils or other materials that may be hazardous in the area or on the floor.		
	III	Is the office area free of unnecessary articles and items?	Are items that are not needed been removed from the work zone, i.e. monitors, scanners, stationary, extra items?		
	IV	Is the office area free of excess consumables/materials?	Evaluate against how many items are in the processing area for work. Assess if the materials, parts, and supplies in the area are currently needed for the job. Closer to actually needed is better.		
	V	Is the information board active?	All announcements are displayed currently and in good presentable shape. Arrangement is straight and placed under appropriate headings.		
	VI	Are the areas walls and dividers free of items not used in the operation?	Extra items are not on the walls, dividers, calendars, or hanging of posters that are not necessary.		
			Category Subtotal		
			Sort Score: Subtotal divided by 6		
SET IN ORDER / STRAIGHTEN	VII	Evaluate any documentation storage.	Only documents required for jobs are stored at the point of use. These documents are stored nicely and in an orderly fashion that is recognizable/understandable to outsiders.		
	VIII	How are the shelves, desks, and work surfaces arranged?	All locations of items are labeled, marked, and it is known if they are missing.		
	IX	How are the tools and materials stored in the area?	No items are resting on walls, tucked in corners. No items are resting on equipment, cupboards, or other fixtures.		
	X	Evaluate container and any packaging locations and tidiness.	Boxes, storage containers, and other items are stored in the appropriate place and orientated well for the area. Cabinets are secure and not causing any danger to the people working in the area.		
	XI	Assess order and where items are found on the floor.	Nothing is sitting directly on the floor and no materials are left around the area. Items that need to be on the floor are clearly marked and positioned in designated areas clearly outlined on the floor.		
	XII	Easiness to access the tools, equipment, and stationary.	Materials, tools, jigs, attachments, and fixtures are organized so that they are all easily within reach. Consider this as well for any kind of tools needed for a job including cutting and measuring something.		
			Category Subtotal		
			Set in Order / Straighten Score: Subtotal divided by 6		
SHINE / SWEEP	XIII	The storage of templates and any tools.	Arrangement of all templates, tools, and materials are kept in clean area for storage and no risk of losing information during movements around office.		
	XIV	Clear when equipment needs maintenance and when last maintained.	Instructions on equipment in the office is marked, highlighted, and labeled. Check sheets available for high value equipment. Maintenance is scheduled for critical equipment.		
	XV	Assess the cleanliness of the office.	How dust free are the areas? This may be critical. Look under desks and behind work spaces to see if there is garbage and other unnecessary items.		
	XVI	Assess status of equipment in the area. Cleanliness overall appearance.	Are machines and equipment known to be on a schedule of cleaning?		
			Category Subtotal		
			Shine / Sweep Score: Subtotal divided by 4		
STANDARDIZE	XVII	Is there visual color diagramming and color coding?	A clear and present color coding system is present in the office and across departments. It is clear that standards are being maintained and improved on.		
	XVIII	Assess the access ways in case of emergency.	All emergency systems; fire vehicles, fire extinguishers, and emergency equipment free of obstruction and clear at all times. Access to electrical controls and fuses are known, marked, and free of any obstructions.		
	XIX	The aisle ways are bright with light and clearly marked.	Walkways are clearly highlighted for direction, aisle access identified at any moment.		
	XX	General area has quantity limits for materials and are marked clearly.	Heights are marked, quantity of materials are known, and min vs. max. This includes paper for machines, number of computers required, toner levels, graphical paper, and special office material needed.		
	XXI	Is there clear document control of information in the office?	All information and documentation is controlled, labeled, and revisions are up to date. There are no label-less binders or pieces of paper in the area.		
			Category Subtotal		
			Standardize Score: Subtotal divided by 5		
SUSTAIN	XXII	The aisle ways are clean and maintenance is clear.	Aisles are never full of anything and are clear for passage. All items and products not stored in the aisle and storage is next to aisle accessible for transportation.		
	XXIII	Illustrations and office layout plans are available to compare against.	5S has a maintenance system that allows for control of change and improvement of 5S in the office. Scoring is kept on each of these items and history is present and visible to support future improvement.		
	XXIV	Ability for shared resources and tools to be set back in place for storage.	No self-discipline is necessary to ensure that all stationary, tools, templates, materials, and shared equipment is put back in the same spot. The effort of putting back should not require organizational skills.		
	XXV	Evaluate the involvement of managers in 5S.	Managers are actively involved in the review process of 5S and are supporting improvement activities of the office.		
			Category Subtotal		
			Sustain Score: Subtotal divided by 4		

Total "Category Subtotals" divide by 25 average 5 S score: TOTAL

5S Office Evaluation Review

Date: _____ Evaluation Area: _____

5S Element	Number	Evaluation Criteria	Rank these items from 1 through 5: 5 being well done	Score (1-5)	Ideas / Suggestions / Comments
SORT	I	Are the aisles and walkways open and clear?	All items that are not necessary or unsafe have been removed from the area used as pathways.		
	II	Is the office area free of any spills of fluids?	Consider whether there are any chemicals, water, oils or other materials that may be hazardous in the area or on the floor.		
	III	Is the office area free of unnecessary articles and items?	Are items that are not needed been removed from the work zone, i.e. monitors, scanners, stationary, extra items?		
	IV	Is the office area free of excess consumables/materials?	Evaluate against how many items are in the processing area for work. Assess if the materials, parts, and supplies in the area are currently needed for the job. Closer to actually needed is better.		
	V	Is the information board active?	All announcements are displayed currently and in good presentable shape. Arrangement is straight and placed under appropriate headings.		
	VI	Are the areas walls and dividers free of items not used in the operation?	Extra items are not on the walls, dividers, calendars, or hanging of posters that are not necessary.		
		Category Subtotal			
		Sort Score: Subtotal divided by 6			
SET IN ORDER / STRAIGHTEN	VII	Evaluate any documentation storage.	Only documents required for jobs are stored at the point of use. These documents are stored nicely and in an orderly fashion that is recognizable/understandable to outsiders.		
	VIII	How are the shelves, desks, and work surfaces arranged?	All locations of items are labeled, marked, and it is known if they are missing.		
	IX	How are the tools and materials stored in the area?	No items are resting on walls, tucked in corners. No items are resting on equipment, cupboards, or other fixtures.		
	X	Evaluate container and any packaging locations and tidiness.	Boxes, storage containers, and other items are stored in the appropriate place and orientated well for the area. Cabinets are secure and not causing any danger to the people working in the area.		
	XI	Assess order and where items are found on the floor.	Nothing is sitting directly on the floor and no materials are left around the area. Items that need to be on the floor are clearly marked and positioned in designated areas clearly outlined on the floor.		
	XII	Easiness to access the tools, equipment, and stationary.	Materials, tools, jigs, attachments, and fixtures are organized so that they are all easily within reach. Consider this as well for any kind of tools needed for a job including cutting and measuring something.		
		Category Subtotal			
		Set in Order / Straighten Score: Subtotal divided by 6			
SHINE / SWEEP	XIII	The storage of templates and any tools.	Arrangement of all templates, tools, and materials are kept in clean area for storage and no risk of losing information during movements around office.		
	XIV	Clear when equipment needs maintenance and when last maintained.	Instructions on equipment in the office is marked, highlighted, and labeled. Check sheets available for high value equipment. Maintenance is scheduled for critical equipment.		
	XV	Assess the cleanliness of the office.	How dust free are the areas? This may be critical. Look under desks and behind work spaces to see if there is garbage and other unnecessary items.		
	XVI	Assess status of equipment in the area. Cleanliness overall appearance.	Are machines and equipment known to be on a schedule of cleaning?		
		Category Subtotal			
		Shine / Sweep Score: Subtotal divided by 4			
STANDARDIZE	XVII	Is there visual color diagramming and color coding?	A clear and present color coding system is present in the office and across departments. It is clear that standards are being maintained and improved on.		
	XVIII	Assess the access ways in case of emergency.	All emergency systems; fire vehicles, fire extinguishers, and emergency equipment free of obstruction and clear at all times. Access to electrical controls and fuses are known, marked, and free of any obstructions.		
	XIX	The aisle ways are bright with light and clearly marked.	Walkways are clearly highlighted for direction, aisle access identified at any moment.		
	XX	General area has quantity limits for materials and are marked clearly.	Heights are marked, quantity of materials are known, and min vs. max. This includes paper for machines, number of computers required, toner levels, graphical paper, and special office material needed.		
	XXI	Is there clear document control of information in the office?	All information and documentation is controlled, labeled, and revisions are up to date. There are no label-less binders or pieces of paper in the area.		
		Category Subtotal			
		Standardize Score: Subtotal divided by 5			
SUSTAIN	XXII	The aisle ways are clean and maintenance is clear.	Aisles are never full of anything and are clear for passage. All items and products not stored in the aisle and storage is next to aisle accessible for transportation.		
	XXIII	Illustrations and office layout plans are available to compare against.	5S has a maintenance system that allows for control of change and improvement of 5S in the office. Scoring is kept on each of these items and history is present and visible to support future improvement.		
	XXIV	Ability for shared resources and tools to be set back in place for storage.	No self-discipline is necessary to ensure that all stationary, tools, templates, materials, and shared equipment is put back in the same spot. The effort of putting back should not require organizational skills.		
	XXV	Evaluate the involvement of managers in 5S.	Managers are actively involved in the review process of 5S and are supporting improvement activities of the office.		
		Category Subtotal			
		Sustain Score: Subtotal divided by 4		**Total "Category Subtotals" divide by 25 average 5 S score: TOTAL**

5S Office Evaluation Review

Date: _____   Evaluation Area: _____

5S Element	Number	Evaluation Criteria	Rank these items from 1 through 5: 5 being well done	Score (1-5)	Ideas / Suggestions / Comments
SORT	I	Are the aisles and walkways open and clear?	All items that are not necessary or unsafe have been removed from the area used as pathways.		
	II	Is the office area free of any spills of fluids?	Consider whether there are any chemicals, water, oils or other materials that may be hazardous in the area or on the floor.		
	III	Is the office area free of unnecessary articles and items?	Are items that are not needed been removed from the work zone, i.e. monitors, scanners, stationary, extra items?		
	IV	Is the office area free of excess consumables/materials?	Evaluate against how many items are in the processing area for work. Assess if the materials, parts, and supplies in the area are currently needed for the job. Closer to actually needed is better.		
	V	Is the information board active?	All announcements are displayed currently and in good presentable shape. Arrangement is straight and placed under appropriate headings.		
	VI	Are the areas walls and dividers free of items not used in the operation?	Extra items are not on the walls, dividers, calendars, or hanging of posters that are not necessary.		
			Category Subtotal		
			Sort Score: Subtotal divided by 6		
SET IN ORDER / STRAIGHTEN	VII	Evaluate any documentation storage.	Only documents required for jobs are stored at the point of use. These documents are stored nicely and in an orderly fashion that is recognizable/understandable to outsiders.		
	VIII	How are the shelves, desks, and work surfaces arranged?	All locations of items are labeled, marked, and it is known if they are missing.		
	IX	How are the tools and materials stored in the area?	No items are resting on walls, tucked in corners. No items are resting on equipment, cupboards, or other fixtures.		
	X	Evaluate container and any packaging locations and tidiness.	Boxes, storage containers, and other items are stored in the appropriate place and orientated well for the area. Cabinets are secure and not causing any danger to the people working in the area.		
	XI	Assess order and where items are found on the floor.	Nothing is sitting directly on the floor and no materials are left around the area. Items that need to be on the floor are clearly marked and positioned in designated areas clearly outlined on the floor.		
	XII	Easiness to access the tools, equipment, and stationary.	Materials, tools, jigs, attachments, and fixtures are organized so that they are all easily within reach. Consider this as well for any kind of tools needed for a job including cutting and measuring something.		
			Category Subtotal		
			Set in Order / Straighten Score: Subtotal divided by 6		
SHINE / SWEEP	XIII	The storage of templates and any tools.	Arrangement of all templates, tools, and materials are kept in clean area for storage and no risk of losing information during movements around office.		
	XIV	Clear when equipment needs maintenance and when last maintained.	Instructions on equipment in the office is marked, highlighted, and labeled. Check sheets available for high value equipment. Maintenance is scheduled for critical equipment.		
	XV	Assess the cleanliness of the office.	How dust free are the areas? This may be critical. Look under desks and behind work spaces to see if there is garbage and other unnecessary items.		
	XVI	Assess status of equipment in the area. Cleanliness overall appearance.	Are machines and equipment known to be on a schedule of cleaning?		
			Category Subtotal		
			Shine / Sweep Score: Subtotal divided by 4		
STANDARDIZE	XVII	Is there visual color diagramming and color coding?	A clear and present color coding system is present in the office and across departments. It is clear that standards are being maintained and improved on.		
	XVIII	Assess the access ways in case of emergency.	All emergency systems; fire vehicles, fire extinguishers, and emergency equipment free of obstruction and clear at all times. Access to electrical controls and fuses are known, marked, and free of any obstructions.		
	XIX	The aisle ways are bright with light and clearly marked.	Walkways are clearly highlighted for direction, aisle access identified at any moment.		
	XX	General area has quantity limits for materials and are marked clearly.	Heights are marked, quantity of materials are known, and min vs. max. This includes paper for machines, number of computers required, toner levels, graphical paper, and special office material needed.		
	XXI	Is there clear document control of information in the office?	All information and documentation is controlled, labeled, and revisions are up to date. There are no label-less binders or pieces of paper in the area.		
			Category Subtotal		
			Standardize Score: Subtotal divided by 5		
SUSTAIN	XXII	The aisle ways are clean and maintenance is clear.	Aisles are never full of anything and are clear for passage. All items and products not stored in the aisle and storage is next to aisle accessible for transportation.		
	XXIII	Illustrations and office layout plans are available to compare against.	5S has a maintenance system that allows for control of change and improvement of 5S in the office. Scoring is kept on each of these items and history is present and visible to support future improvement.		
	XXIV	Ability for shared resources and tools to be set back in place for storage.	No self-discipline is necessary to ensure that all stationary, tools, templates, materials, and shared equipment is put back in the same spot. The effort of putting back should not require organizational skills.		
	XXV	Evaluate the involvement of managers in 5S.	Managers are actively involved in the review process of 5S and are supporting improvement activities of the office.		
			Category Subtotal		
			Sustain Score: Subtotal divided by 4		Total "Category Subtotals" divide by 25 average 5 S score: TOTAL

5S Office Evaluation Review

Date: _____   Evaluation Area: _____

5S Element	Number	Evaluation Criteria	Rank these items from 1 through 5: 5 being well done	Score (1-5)	Ideas / Suggestions / Comments
SORT	I	Are the aisles and walkways open and clear?	All items that are not necessary or unsafe have been removed from the area used as pathways.		
	II	Is the office area free of any spills of fluids?	Consider whether there are any chemicals, water, oils or other materials that may be hazardous in the area or on the floor.		
	III	Is the office area free of unnecessary articles and items?	Are items that are not needed been removed from the work zone, i.e. monitors, scanners, stationary, extra items?		
	IV	Is the office area free of excess consumables/materials?	Evaluate against how many items are in the processing area for work. Assess if the materials, parts, and supplies in the area are currently needed for the job. Closer to actually needed is better.		
	V	Is the information board active?	All announcements are displayed currently and in good presentable shape. Arrangement is straight and placed under appropriate headings.		
	VI	Are the areas walls and dividers free of items not used in the operation?	Extra items are not on the walls, dividers, calendars, or hanging of posters that are not necessary.		
			Category Subtotal		
			Sort Score: Subtotal divided by 6		
SET IN ORDER / STRAIGHTEN	VII	Evaluate any documentation storage.	Only documents required for jobs are stored at the point of use. These documents are stored nicely and in an orderly fashion that is recognizable/understandable to outsiders.		
	VIII	How are the shelves, desks, and work surfaces arranged?	All locations of items are labeled, marked, and it is known if they are missing.		
	IX	How are the tools and materials stored in the area?	No items are resting on walls, tucked in corners. No items are resting on equipment, cupboards, or other fixtures.		
	X	Evaluate container and any packaging locations and tidiness.	Boxes, storage containers, and other items are stored in the appropriate place and orientated well for the area. Cabinets are secure and not causing any danger to the people working in the area.		
	XI	Assess order and where items are found on the floor.	Nothing is sitting directly on the floor and no materials are left around the area. Items that need to be on the floor are clearly marked and positioned in designated areas clearly outlined on the floor.		
	XII	Easiness to access the tools, equipment, and stationary.	Materials, tools, jigs, attachments, and fixtures are organized so that they are all easily within reach. Consider this as well for any kind of tools needed for a job including cutting and measuring something.		
			Category Subtotal		
			Set in Order / Straighten Score: Subtotal divided by 6		
SHINE / SWEEP	XIII	The storage of templates and any tools.	Arrangement of all templates, tools, and materials are kept in clean area for storage and no risk of losing information during movements around office.		
	XIV	Clear when equipment needs maintenance and when last maintained.	Instructions on equipment in the office is marked, highlighted, and labeled. Check sheets available for high value equipment. Maintenance is scheduled for critical equipment.		
	XV	Assess the cleanliness of the office.	How dust free are the areas? This may be critical. Look under desks and behind work spaces to see if there is garbage and other unnecessary items.		
	XVI	Assess status of equipment in the area. Cleanliness overall appearance.	Are machines and equipment known to be on a schedule of cleaning?		
			Category Subtotal		
			Shine / Sweep Score: Subtotal divided by 4		
STANDARDIZE	XVII	Is there visual color diagramming and color coding?	A clear and present color coding system is present in the office and across departments. It is clear that standards are being maintained and improved on.		
	XVIII	Assess the access ways in case of emergency.	All emergency systems; fire vehicles, fire extinguishers, and emergency equipment free of obstruction and clear at all times. Access to electrical controls and fuses are known, marked, and free of any obstructions.		
	XIX	The aisle ways are bright with light and clearly marked.	Walkways are clearly highlighted for direction, aisle access identified at any moment.		
	XX	General area has quantity limits for materials and are marked clearly.	Heights are marked, quantity of materials are known, and min vs. max. This includes paper for machines, number of computers required, toner levels, graphical paper, and special office material needed.		
	XXI	Is there clear document control of information in the office?	All information and documentation is controlled, labeled, and revisions are up to date. There are no label-less binders or pieces of paper in the area.		
			Category Subtotal		
			Standardize Score: Subtotal divided by 5		
SUSTAIN	XXII	The aisle ways are clean and maintenance is clear.	Aisles are never full of anything and are clear for passage. All items and products not stored in the aisle and storage is next to aisle accessible for transportation.		
	XXIII	Illustrations and office layout plans are available to compare against.	5S has a maintenance system that allows for control of change and improvement of 5S in the office. Scoring is kept on each of these items and history is present and visible to support future improvement.		
	XXIV	Ability for shared resources and tools to be set back in place for storage.	No self-discipline is necessary to ensure that all stationary, tools, templates, materials, and shared equipment is put back in the same spot. The effort of putting back should not require organizational skills.		
	XXV	Evaluate the involvement of managers in 5S.	Managers are actively involved in the review process of 5S and are supporting improvement activities of the office.		
			Category Subtotal		
			Sustain Score: Subtotal divided by 4		

Total "Category Subtotals" divide by 25 average 5 S score: TOTAL

5S Office Evaluation Review

Date: _____   Evaluation Area: _____

5S Element	Number	Evaluation Criteria	Rank these items from 1 through 5: 5 being well done	Score (1-5)	Ideas / Suggestions / Comments
SORT	I	Are the aisles and walkways open and clear?	All items that are not necessary or unsafe have been removed from the area used as pathways.		
	II	Is the office area free of any spills of fluids?	Consider whether there are any chemicals, water, oils or other materials that may be hazardous in the area or on the floor.		
	III	Is the office area free of unnecessary articles and items?	Are items that are not needed been removed from the work zone, i.e. monitors, scanners, stationary, extra items?		
	IV	Is the office area free of excess consumables/materials?	Evaluate against how many items are in the processing area for work. Assess if the materials, parts, and supplies in the area are currently needed for the job. Closer to actually needed is better.		
	V	Is the information board active?	All announcements are displayed currently and in good presentable shape. Arrangement is straight and placed under appropriate headings.		
	VI	Are the areas walls and dividers free of items not used in the operation?	Extra items are not on the walls, dividers, calendars, or hanging of posters that are not necessary.		
			Category Subtotal	- - - -	
			Sort Score: Subtotal divided by 6		
SET IN ORDER / STRAIGHTEN	VII	Evaluate any documentation storage.	Only documents required for jobs are stored at the point of use. These documents are stored nicely and in an orderly fashion that is recognizable/understandable to outsiders.		
	VIII	How are the shelves, desks, and work surfaces arranged?	All locations of items are labeled, marked, and it is known if they are missing.		
	IX	How are the tools and materials stored in the area?	No items are resting on walls, tucked in corners. No items are resting on equipment, cupboards, or other fixtures.		
	X	Evaluate container and any packaging locations and tidiness.	Boxes, storage containers, and other items are stored in the appropriate place and orientated well for the area. Cabinets are secure and not causing any danger to the people working in the area.		
	XI	Assess order and where items are found on the floor.	Nothing is sitting directly on the floor and no materials are left around the area. Items that need to be on the floor are clearly marked and positioned in designated areas clearly outlined on the floor.		
	XII	Easiness to access the tools, equipment, and stationary.	Materials, tools, jigs, attachments, and fixtures are organized so that they are all easily within reach. Consider this as well for any kind of tools needed for a job including cutting and measuring something.		
			Category Subtotal	- - - -	
			Set in Order / Straighten Score: Subtotal divided by 6		
SHINE / SWEEP	XIII	The storage of templates and any tools.	Arrangement of all templates, tools, and materials are kept in clean area for storage and no risk of losing information during movements around office.		
	XIV	Clear when equipment needs maintenance and when last maintained.	Instructions on equipment in the office is marked, highlighted, and labeled. Check sheets available for high value equipment. Maintenance is scheduled for critical equipment.		
	XV	Assess the cleanliness of the office.	How dust free are the areas? This may be critical. Look under desks and behind work spaces to see if there is garbage and other unnecessary items.		
	XVI	Assess status of equipment in the area. Cleanliness overall appearance.	Are machines and equipment known to be on a schedule of cleaning?		
			Category Subtotal	- - - -	
			Shine / Sweep Score: Subtotal divided by 4		
STANDARDIZE	XVII	Is there visual color diagramming and color coding?	A clear and present color coding system is present in the office and across departments. It is clear that standards are being maintained and improved on.		
	XVIII	Assess the access ways in case of emergency.	All emergency systems; fire vehicles, fire extinguishers, and emergency equipment free of obstruction and clear at all times. Access to electrical controls and fuses are known, marked, and free of any obstructions.		
	XIX	The aisle ways are bright with light and clearly marked.	Walkways are clearly highlighted for direction, aisle access identified at any moment.		
	XX	General area has quantity limits for materials and are marked clearly.	Heights are marked, quantity of materials are known, and min vs. max. This includes paper for machines, number of computers required, toner levels, graphical paper, and special office material needed.		
	XXI	Is there clear document control of information in the office?	All information and documentation is controlled, labeled, and revisions are up to date. There are no label-less binders or pieces of paper in the area.		
			Category Subtotal	- - - -	
			Standardize Score: Subtotal divided by 5		
SUSTAIN	XXII	The aisle ways are clean and maintenance is clear.	Aisles are never full of anything and are clear for passage. All items and products not stored in the aisle and storage is next to aisle accessible for transportation.		
	XXIII	Illustrations and office layout plans are available to compare against.	5S has a maintenance system that allows for control of change and improvement of 5S in the office. Scoring is kept on each of these items and history is present and visible to support future improvement.		
	XXIV	Ability for shared resources and tools to be set back in place for storage.	No self-discipline is necessary to ensure that all stationary, tools, templates, materials, and shared equipment is put back in the same spot. The effort of putting back should not require organizational skills.		
	XXV	Evaluate the involvement of managers in 5S.	Managers are actively involved in the review process of 5S and are supporting improvement activities of the office.		
			Category Subtotal	- - - -	
			Sustain Score: Subtotal divided by 4		**Total "Category Subtotals" divide by 25 average 5 S score: TOTAL**

5S Office Evaluation Review

Date: _____   Evaluation Area: _____

5S Element	Number	Evaluation Criteria	Rank these items from 1 through 5: 5 being well done	Score (1-5)	Ideas / Suggestions / Comments
SORT	I	Are the aisles and walkways open and clear?	All items that are not necessary or unsafe have been removed from the area used as pathways.		
	II	Is the office area free of any spills of fluids?	Consider whether there are any chemicals, water, oils or other materials that may be hazardous in the area or on the floor.		
	III	Is the office area free of unnecessary articles and items?	Are items that are not needed been removed from the work zone, i.e. monitors, scanners, stationary, extra items?		
	IV	Is the office area free of excess consumables/materials?	Evaluate against how many items are in the processing area for work. Assess if the materials, parts, and supplies in the area are currently needed for the job. Closer to actually needed is better.		
	V	Is the information board active?	All announcements are displayed currently and in good presentable shape. Arrangement is straight and placed under appropriate headings.		
	VI	Are the areas walls and dividers free of items not used in the operation?	Extra items are not on the walls, dividers, calendars, or hanging of posters that are not necessary.		
			Category Subtotal		
			Sort Score: Subtotal divided by 6		
SET IN ORDER / STRAIGHTEN	VII	Evaluate any documentation storage.	Only documents required for jobs are stored at the point of use. These documents are stored nicely and in an orderly fashion that is recognizable/understandable to outsiders.		
	VIII	How are the shelves, desks, and work surfaces arranged?	All locations of items are labeled, marked, and it is known if they are missing.		
	IX	How are the tools and materials stored in the area?	No items are resting on walls, tucked in corners. No items are resting on equipment, cupboards, or other fixtures.		
	X	Evaluate container and any packaging locations and tidiness.	Boxes, storage containers, and other items are stored in the appropriate place and orientated well for the area. Cabinets are secure and not causing any danger to the people working in the area.		
	XI	Assess order and where items are found on the floor.	Nothing is sitting directly on the floor and no materials are left around the area. Items that need to be on the floor are clearly marked and positioned in designated areas clearly outlined on the floor.		
	XII	Easiness to access the tools, equipment, and stationary.	Materials, tools, jigs, attachments, and fixtures are organized so that they are all easily within reach. Consider this as well for any kind of tools needed for a job including cutting and measuring something.		
			Category Subtotal		
			Set in Order / Straighten Score: Subtotal divided by 6		
SHINE / SWEEP	XIII	The storage of templates and any tools.	Arrangement of all templates, tools, and materials are kept in clean area for storage and no risk of losing information during movements around office.		
	XIV	Clear when equipment needs maintenance and when last maintained.	Instructions on equipment in the office is marked, highlighted, and labeled. Check sheets available for high value equipment. Maintenance is scheduled for critical equipment.		
	XV	Assess the cleanliness of the office.	How dust free are the areas? This may be critical. Look under desks and behind work spaces to see if there is garbage and other unnecessary items.		
	XVI	Assess status of equipment in the area. Cleanliness overall appearance.	Are machines and equipment known to be on a schedule of cleaning?		
			Category Subtotal		
			Shine / Sweep Score: Subtotal divided by 4		
STANDARDIZE	XVII	Is there visual color diagramming and color coding?	A clear and present color coding system is present in the office and across departments. It is clear that standards are being maintained and improved on.		
	XVIII	Assess the access ways in case of emergency.	All emergency systems; fire vehicles, fire extinguishers, and emergency equipment free of obstruction and clear at all times. Access to electrical controls and fuses are known, marked, and free of any obstructions.		
	XIX	The aisle ways are bright with light and clearly marked.	Walkways are clearly highlighted for direction, aisle access identified at any moment.		
	XX	General area has quantity limits for materials and are marked clearly.	Heights are marked, quantity of materials are known, and min vs. max. This includes paper for machines, number of computers required, toner levels, graphical paper, and special office material needed.		
	XXI	Is there clear document control of information in the office?	All information and documentation is controlled, labeled, and revisions are up to date. There are no label-less binders or pieces of paper in the area.		
			Category Subtotal		
			Standardize Score: Subtotal divided by 5		
SUSTAIN	XXII	The aisle ways are clean and maintenance is clear.	Aisles are never full of anything and are clear for passage. All items and products not stored in the aisle and storage is next to aisle accessible for transportation.		
	XXIII	Illustrations and office layout plans are available to compare against.	5S has a maintenance system that allows for control of change and improvement of 5S in the office. Scoring is kept on each of these items and history is present and visible to support future improvement.		
	XXIV	Ability for shared resources and tools to be set back in place for storage.	No self-discipline is necessary to ensure that all stationary, tools, templates, materials, and shared equipment is put back in the same spot. The effort of putting back should not require organizational skills.		
	XXV	Evaluate the involvement of managers in 5S.	Managers are actively involved in the review process of 5S and are supporting improvement activities of the office.		
			Category Subtotal		
			Sustain Score: Subtotal divided by 4		Total "Category Subtotals" divide by 25 average 5 S score: TOTAL

5S Office Evaluation Review

Date: _____   Evaluation Area: _____

5S Element	Number	Evaluation Criteria	Rank these items from 1 through 5: 5 being well done	Score (1-5)	Ideas / Suggestions / Comments
SORT	I	Are the aisles and walkways open and clear?	All items that are not necessary or unsafe have been removed from the area used as pathways.		
	II	Is the office area free of any spills of fluids?	Consider whether there are any chemicals, water, oils or other materials that may be hazardous in the area or on the floor.		
	III	Is the office area free of unnecessary articles and items?	Are items that are not needed been removed from the work zone, i.e. monitors, scanners, stationary, extra items?		
	IV	Is the office area free of excess consumables/materials?	Evaluate against how many items are in the processing area for work. Assess if the materials, parts, and supplies in the area are currently needed for the job. Closer to actually needed is better.		
	V	Is the information board active?	All announcements are displayed currently and in good presentable shape. Arrangement is straight and placed under appropriate headings.		
	VI	Are the areas walls and dividers free of items not used in the operation?	Extra items are not on the walls, dividers, calendars, or hanging of posters that are not necessary.		
			Category Subtotal		
			Sort Score: Subtotal divided by 6		
SET IN ORDER / STRAIGHTEN	VII	Evaluate any documentation storage.	Only documents required for jobs are stored at the point of use. These documents are stored nicely and in an orderly fashion that is recognizable/understandable to outsiders.		
	VIII	How are the shelves, desks, and work surfaces arranged?	All locations of items are labeled, marked, and it is known if they are missing.		
	IX	How are the tools and materials stored in the area?	No items are resting on walls, tucked in corners. No items are resting on equipment, cupboards, or other fixtures.		
	X	Evaluate container and any packaging locations and tidiness.	Boxes, storage containers, and other items are stored in the appropriate place and orientated well for the area. Cabinets are secure and not causing any danger to the people working in the area.		
	XI	Assess order and where items are found on the floor.	Nothing is sitting directly on the floor and no materials are left around the area. Items that need to be on the floor are clearly marked and positioned in designated areas clearly outlined on the floor.		
	XII	Easiness to access the tools, equipment, and stationary.	Materials, tools, jigs, attachments, and fixtures are organized so that they are all easily within reach. Consider this as well for any kind of tools needed for a job including cutting and measuring something.		
			Category Subtotal		
			Set in Order / Straighten Score: Subtotal divided by 6		
SHINE / SWEEP	XIII	The storage of templates and any tools.	Arrangement of all templates, tools, and materials are kept in clean area for storage and no risk of losing information during movements around office.		
	XIV	Clear when equipment needs maintenance and when last maintained.	Instructions on equipment in the office is marked, highlighted, and labeled. Check sheets available for high value equipment. Maintenance is scheduled for critical equipment.		
	XV	Assess the cleanliness of the office.	How dust free are the areas? This may be critical. Look under desks and behind work spaces to see if there is garbage and other unnecessary items.		
	XVI	Assess status of equipment in the area. Cleanliness overall appearance.	Are machines and equipment known to be on a schedule of cleaning?		
			Category Subtotal		
			Shine / Sweep Score: Subtotal divided by 4		
STANDARDIZE	XVII	Is there visual color diagramming and color coding?	A clear and present color coding system is present in the office and across departments. It is clear that standards are being maintained and improved on.		
	XVIII	Assess the access ways in case of emergency.	All emergency systems; fire vehicles, fire extinguishers, and emergency equipment free of obstruction and clear at all times. Access to electrical controls and fuses are known, marked, and free of any obstructions.		
	XIX	The aisle ways are bright with light and clearly marked.	Walkways are clearly highlighted for direction, aisle access identified at any moment.		
	XX	General area has quantity limits for materials and are marked clearly.	Heights are marked, quantity of materials are known, and min vs. max. This includes paper for machines, number of computers required, toner levels, graphical paper, and special office material needed.		
	XXI	Is there clear document control of information in the office?	All information and documentation is controlled, labeled, and revisions are up to date. There are no label-less binders or pieces of paper in the area.		
			Category Subtotal		
			Standardize Score: Subtotal divided by 5		
SUSTAIN	XXII	The aisle ways are clean and maintenance is clear.	Aisles are never full of anything and are clear for passage. All items and products not stored in the aisle and storage is next to aisle accessible for transportation.		
	XXIII	Illustrations and office layout plans are available to compare against.	5S has a maintenance system that allows for control of change and improvement of 5S in the office. Scoring is kept on each of these items and history is present and visible to support future improvement.		
	XXIV	Ability for shared resources and tools to be set back in place for storage.	No self-discipline is necessary to ensure that all stationary, tools, templates, materials, and shared equipment is put back in the same spot. The effort of putting back should not require organizational skills.		
	XXV	Evaluate the involvement of managers in 5S.	Managers are actively involved in the review process of 5S and are supporting improvement activities of the office.		
			Category Subtotal		
			Sustain Score: Subtotal divided by 4		**Total "Category Subtotals" divide by 25 average 5 S score: TOTAL**

5S Office Evaluation Review

Date: _____   Evaluation Area: _____

5S Element	Number	Evaluation Criteria	Rank these items from 1 through 5: 5 being well done	Score (1-5)	Ideas / Suggestions / Comments
SORT	I	Are the aisles and walkways open and clear?	All items that are not necessary or unsafe have been removed from the area used as pathways.		
	II	Is the office area free of any spills of fluids?	Consider whether there are any chemicals, water, oils or other materials that may be hazardous in the area or on the floor.		
	III	Is the office area free of unnecessary articles and items?	Are items that are not needed been removed from the work zone, i.e. monitors, scanners, stationary, extra items?		
	IV	Is the office area free of excess consumables/materials?	Evaluate against how many items are in the processing area for work. Assess if the materials, parts, and supplies in the area are currently needed for the job. Closer to actually needed is better.		
	V	Is the information board active?	All announcements are displayed currently and in good presentable shape. Arrangement is straight and placed under appropriate headings.		
	VI	Are the areas walls and dividers free of items not used in the operation?	Extra items are not on the walls, dividers, calendars, or hanging of posters that are not necessary.		
			Category Subtotal		
			Sort Score: Subtotal divided by 6		
SET IN ORDER / STRAIGHTEN	VII	Evaluate any documentation storage.	Only documents required for jobs are stored at the point of use. These documents are stored nicely and in an orderly fashion that is recognizable/understandable to outsiders.		
	VIII	How are the shelves, desks, and work surfaces arranged?	All locations of items are labeled, marked, and it is known if they are missing.		
	IX	How are the tools and materials stored in the area?	No items are resting on walls, tucked in corners. No items are resting on equipment, cupboards, or other fixtures.		
	X	Evaluate container and any packaging locations and tidiness.	Boxes, storage containers, and other items are stored in the appropriate place and orientated well for the area. Cabinets are secure and not causing any danger to the people working in the area.		
	XI	Assess order and where items are found on the floor.	Nothing is sitting directly on the floor and no materials are left around the area. Items that need to be on the floor are clearly marked and positioned in designated areas clearly outlined on the floor.		
	XII	Easiness to access the tools, equipment, and stationary.	Materials, tools, jigs, attachments, and fixtures are organized so that they are all easily within reach. Consider this as well for any kind of tools needed for a job including cutting and measuring something.		
			Category Subtotal		
			Set in Order / Straighten Score: Subtotal divided by 6		
SHINE / SWEEP	XIII	The storage of templates and any tools.	Arrangement of all templates, tools, and materials are kept in clean area for storage and no risk of losing information during movements around office.		
	XIV	Clear when equipment needs maintenance and when last maintained.	Instructions on equipment in the office is marked, highlighted, and labeled. Check sheets available for high value equipment. Maintenance is scheduled for critical equipment.		
	XV	Assess the cleanliness of the office.	How dust free are the areas? This may be critical. Look under desks and behind work spaces to see if there is garbage and other unnecessary items.		
	XVI	Assess status of equipment in the area. Cleanliness overall appearance.	Are machines and equipment known to be on a schedule of cleaning?		
			Category Subtotal		
			Shine / Sweep Score: Subtotal divided by 4		
STANDARDIZE	XVII	Is there visual color diagramming and color coding?	A clear and present color coding system is present in the office and across departments. It is clear that standards are being maintained and improved on.		
	XVIII	Assess the access ways in case of emergency.	All emergency systems; fire vehicles, fire extinguishers, and emergency equipment free of obstruction and clear at all times. Access to electrical controls and fuses are known, marked, and free of any obstructions.		
	XIX	The aisle ways are bright with light and clearly marked.	Walkways are clearly highlighted for direction, aisle access identified at any moment.		
	XX	General area has quantity limits for materials and are marked clearly.	Heights are marked, quantity of materials are known, and min vs. max. This includes paper for machines, number of computers required, toner levels, graphical paper, and special office material needed.		
	XXI	Is there clear document control of information in the office?	All information and documentation is controlled, labeled, and revisions are up to date. There are no label-less binders or pieces of paper in the area.		
			Category Subtotal		
			Standardize Score: Subtotal divided by 5		
SUSTAIN	XXII	The aisle ways are clean and maintenance is clear.	Aisles are never full of anything and are clear for passage. All items and products not stored in the aisle and storage is next to aisle accessible for transportation.		
	XXIII	Illustrations and office layout plans are available to compare against.	5S has a maintenance system that allows for control of change and improvement of 5S in the office. Scoring is kept on each of these items and history is present and visible to support future improvement.		
	XXIV	Ability for shared resources and tools to be set back in place for storage.	No self-discipline is necessary to ensure that all stationary, tools, templates, materials, and shared equipment is put back in the same spot. The effort of putting back should not require organizational skills.		
	XXV	Evaluate the involvement of managers in 5S.	Managers are actively involved in the review process of 5S and are supporting improvement activities of the office.		
			Category Subtotal		
			Sustain Score: Subtotal divided by 4		

Total "Category Subtotals" divide by 25 average 5 S score: TOTAL

5S Office Evaluation Review

Date: _____   Evaluation Area: _____

5S Element	Number	Evaluation Criteria	Rank these items from 1 through 5: 5 being well done	Score (1-5)	Ideas / Suggestions / Comments
SORT	I	Are the aisles and walkways open and clear?	All items that are not necessary or unsafe have been removed from the area used as pathways.		
	II	Is the office area free of any spills of fluids?	Consider whether there are any chemicals, water, oils or other materials that may be hazardous in the area or on the floor.		
	III	Is the office area free of unnecessary articles and items?	Are items that are not needed been removed from the work zone, i.e. monitors, scanners, stationary, extra items?		
	IV	Is the office area free of excess consumables/materials?	Evaluate against how many items are in the processing area for work. Assess if the materials, parts, and supplies in the area are currently needed for the job. Closer to actually needed is better.		
	V	Is the information board active?	All announcements are displayed currently and in good presentable shape. Arrangement is straight and placed under appropriate headings.		
	VI	Are the areas walls and dividers free of items not used in the operation?	Extra items are not on the walls, dividers, calendars, or hanging of posters that are not necessary.		
			Category Subtotal		
			Sort Score: Subtotal divided by 6		
SET IN ORDER / STRAIGHTEN	VII	Evaluate any documentation storage.	Only documents required for jobs are stored at the point of use. These documents are stored nicely and in an orderly fashion that is recognizable/understandable to outsiders.		
	VIII	How are the shelves, desks, and work surfaces arranged?	All locations of items are labeled, marked, and it is known if they are missing.		
	IX	How are the tools and materials stored in the area?	No items are resting on walls, tucked in corners. No items are resting on equipment, cupboards, or other fixtures.		
	X	Evaluate container and any packaging locations and tidiness.	Boxes, storage containers, and other items are stored in the appropriate place and orientated well for the area. Cabinets are secure and not causing any danger to the people working in the area.		
	XI	Assess order and where items are found on the floor.	Nothing is sitting directly on the floor and no materials are left around the area. Items that need to be on the floor are clearly marked and positioned in designated areas clearly outlined on the floor.		
	XII	Easiness to access the tools, equipment, and stationary.	Materials, tools, jigs, attachments, and fixtures are organized so that they are all easily within reach. Consider this as well for any kind of tools needed for a job including cutting and measuring something.		
			Category Subtotal		
			Set in Order / Straighten Score: Subtotal divided by 6		
SHINE / SWEEP	XIII	The storage of templates and any tools.	Arrangement of all templates, tools, and materials are kept in clean area for storage and no risk of losing information during movements around office.		
	XIV	Clear when equipment needs maintenance and when last maintained.	Instructions on equipment in the office is marked, highlighted, and labeled. Check sheets available for high value equipment. Maintenance is scheduled for critical equipment.		
	XV	Assess the cleanliness of the office.	How dust free are the areas? This may be critical. Look under desks and behind work spaces to see if there is garbage and other unnecessary items.		
	XVI	Assess status of equipment in the area. Cleanliness overall appearance.	Are machines and equipment known to be on a schedule of cleaning?		
			Category Subtotal		
			Shine / Sweep Score: Subtotal divided by 4		
STANDARDIZE	XVII	Is there visual color diagramming and color coding?	A clear and present color coding system is present in the office and across departments. It is clear that standards are being maintained and improved on.		
	XVIII	Assess the access ways in case of emergency.	All emergency systems; fire vehicles, fire extinguishers, and emergency equipment free of obstruction and clear at all times. Access to electrical controls and fuses are known, marked, and free of any obstructions.		
	XIX	The aisle ways are bright with light and clearly marked.	Walkways are clearly highlighted for direction, aisle access identified at any moment.		
	XX	General area has quantity limits for materials and are marked clearly.	Heights are marked, quantity of materials are known, and min vs. max. This includes paper for machines, number of computers required, toner levels, graphical paper, and special office material needed.		
	XXI	Is there clear document control of information in the office?	All information and documentation is controlled, labeled, and revisions are up to date. There are no label-less binders or pieces of paper in the area.		
			Category Subtotal		
			Standardize Score: Subtotal divided by 5		
SUSTAIN	XXII	The aisle ways are clean and maintenance is clear.	Aisles are never full of anything and are clear for passage. All items and products not stored in the aisle and storage is next to aisle accessible for transportation.		
	XXIII	Illustrations and office layout plans are available to compare against.	5S has a maintenance system that allows for control of change and improvement of 5S in the office. Scoring is kept on each of these items and history is present and visible to support future improvement.		
	XXIV	Ability for shared resources and tools to be set back in place for storage.	No self-discipline is necessary to ensure that all stationary, tools, templates, materials, and shared equipment is put back in the same spot. The effort of putting back should not require organizational skills.		
	XXV	Evaluate the involvement of managers in 5S.	Managers are actively involved in the review process of 5S and are supporting improvement activities of the office.		
			Category Subtotal		
			Sustain Score: Subtotal divided by 4		

Total "Category Subtotals" divide by 25 average 5 S score: TOTAL

5S Office Evaluation Review

Date: _____   Evaluation Area: _____

5S Element	Number	Evaluation Criteria	Rank these items from 1 through 5: 5 being well done	Score (1-5)	Ideas / Suggestions / Comments
SORT	I	Are the aisles and walkways open and clear?	All items that are not necessary or unsafe have been removed from the area used as pathways.		
	II	Is the office area free of any spills of fluids?	Consider whether there are any chemicals, water, oils or other materials that may be hazardous in the area or on the floor.		
	III	Is the office area free of unnecessary articles and items?	Are items that are not needed been removed from the work zone, i.e. monitors, scanners, stationary, extra items?		
	IV	Is the office area free of excess consumables/materials?	Evaluate against how many items are in the processing area for work. Assess if the materials, parts, and supplies in the area are currently needed for the job. Closer to actually needed is better.		
	V	Is the information board active?	All announcements are displayed currently and in good presentable shape. Arrangement is straight and placed under appropriate headings.		
	VI	Are the areas walls and dividers free of items not used in the operation?	Extra items are not on the walls, dividers, calendars, or hanging of posters that are not necessary.		
			Category Subtotal		
			Sort Score: Subtotal divided by 6		
SET IN ORDER / STRAIGHTEN	VII	Evaluate any documentation storage.	Only documents required for jobs are stored at the point of use. These documents are stored nicely and in an orderly fashion that is recognizable/understandable to outsiders.		
	VIII	How are the shelves, desks, and work surfaces arranged?	All locations of items are labeled, marked, and it is known if they are missing.		
	IX	How are the tools and materials stored in the area?	No items are resting on walls, tucked in corners. No items are resting on equipment, cupboards, or other fixtures.		
	X	Evaluate container and any packaging locations and tidiness.	Boxes, storage containers, and other items are stored in the appropriate place and orientated well for the area. Cabinets are secure and not causing any danger to the people working in the area.		
	XI	Assess order and where items are found on the floor.	Nothing is sitting directly on the floor and no materials are left around the area. Items that need to be on the floor are clearly marked and positioned in designated areas clearly outlined on the floor.		
	XII	Easiness to access the tools, equipment, and stationary.	Materials, tools, jigs, attachments, and fixtures are organized so that they are all easily within reach. Consider this as well for any kind of tools needed for a job including cutting and measuring something.		
			Category Subtotal		
			Set in Order / Straighten Score: Subtotal divided by 6		
SHINE / SWEEP	XIII	The storage of templates and any tools.	Arrangement of all templates, tools, and materials are kept in clean area for storage and no risk of losing information during movements around office.		
	XIV	Clear when equipment needs maintenance and when last maintained.	Instructions on equipment in the office is marked, highlighted, and labeled. Check sheets available for high value equipment. Maintenance is scheduled for critical equipment.		
	XV	Assess the cleanliness of the office.	How dust free are the areas? This may be critical. Look under desks and behind work spaces to see if there is garbage and other unnecessary items.		
	XVI	Assess status of equipment in the area. Cleanliness overall appearance.	Are machines and equipment known to be on a schedule of cleaning?		
			Category Subtotal		
			Shine / Sweep Score: Subtotal divided by 4		
STANDARDIZE	XVII	Is there visual color diagramming and color coding?	A clear and present color coding system is present in the office and across departments. It is clear that standards are being maintained and improved on.		
	XVIII	Assess the access ways in case of emergency.	All emergency systems; fire vehicles, fire extinguishers, and emergency equipment free of obstruction and clear at all times. Access to electrical controls and fuses are known, marked, and free of any obstructions.		
	XIX	The aisle ways are bright with light and clearly marked.	Walkways are clearly highlighted for direction, aisle access identified at any moment.		
	XX	General area has quantity limits for materials and are marked clearly.	Heights are marked, quantity of materials are known, and min vs. max. This includes paper for machines, number of computers required, toner levels, graphical paper, and special office material needed.		
	XXI	Is there clear document control of information in the office?	All information and documentation is controlled, labeled, and revisions are up to date. There are no label-less binders or pieces of paper in the area.		
			Category Subtotal		
			Standardize Score: Subtotal divided by 5		
SUSTAIN	XXII	The aisle ways are clean and maintenance is clear.	Aisles are never full of anything and are clear for passage. All items and products not stored in the aisle and storage is next to aisle accessible for transportation.		
	XXIII	Illustrations and office layout plans are available to compare against.	5S has a maintenance system that allows for control of change and improvement of 5S in the office. Scoring is kept on each of these items and history is present and visible to support future improvement.		
	XXIV	Ability for shared resources and tools to be set back in place for storage.	No self-discipline is necessary to ensure that all stationary, tools, templates, materials, and shared equipment is put back in the same spot. The effort of putting back should not require organizational skills.		
	XXV	Evaluate the involvement of managers in 5S.	Managers are actively involved in the review process of 5S and are supporting improvement activities of the office.		
			Category Subtotal		
			Sustain Score: Subtotal divided by 4		Total "Category Subtotals" divide by 25 average 5 S score: TOTAL

5S Office Evaluation Review

Date: _____   Evaluation Area: _____

5S Element	Number	Evaluation Criteria	Rank these items from 1 through 5: 5 being well done	Score (1-5)	Ideas / Suggestions / Comments
SORT	I	Are the aisles and walkways open and clear?	All items that are not necessary or unsafe have been removed from the area used as pathways.		
	II	Is the office area free of any spills of fluids?	Consider whether there are any chemicals, water, oils or other materials that may be hazardous in the area or on the floor.		
	III	Is the office area free of unnecessary articles and items?	Are items that are not needed been removed from the work zone, i.e. monitors, scanners, stationary, extra items?		
	IV	Is the office area free of excess consumables/materials?	Evaluate against how many items are in the processing area for work. Assess if the materials, parts, and supplies in the area are currently needed for the job. Closer to actually needed is better.		
	V	Is the information board active?	All announcements are displayed currently and in good presentable shape. Arrangement is straight and placed under appropriate headings.		
	VI	Are the areas walls and dividers free of items not used in the operation?	Extra items are not on the walls, dividers, calendars, or hanging of posters that are not necessary.		
			Category Subtotal		
			Sort Score: Subtotal divided by 6		
SET IN ORDER / STRAIGHTEN	VII	Evaluate any documentation storage.	Only documents required for jobs are stored at the point of use. These documents are stored nicely and in an orderly fashion that is recognizable/understandable to outsiders.		
	VIII	How are the shelves, desks, and work surfaces arranged?	All locations of items are labeled, marked, and it is known if they are missing.		
	IX	How are the tools and materials stored in the area?	No items are resting on walls, tucked in corners. No items are resting on equipment, cupboards, or other fixtures.		
	X	Evaluate container and any packaging locations and tidiness.	Boxes, storage containers, and other items are stored in the appropriate place and orientated well for the area. Cabinets are secure and not causing any danger to the people working in the area.		
	XI	Assess order and where items are found on the floor.	Nothing is sitting directly on the floor and no materials are left around the area. Items that need to be on the floor are clearly marked and positioned in designated areas clearly outlined on the floor.		
	XII	Easiness to access the tools, equipment, and stationary.	Materials, tools, jigs, attachments, and fixtures are organized so that they are all easily within reach. Consider this as well for any kind of tools needed for a job including cutting and measuring something.		
			Category Subtotal		
			Set in Order / Straighten Score: Subtotal divided by 6		
SHINE / SWEEP	XIII	The storage of templates and any tools.	Arrangement of all templates, tools, and materials are kept in clean area for storage and no risk of losing information during movements around office.		
	XIV	Clear when equipment needs maintenance and when last maintained.	Instructions on equipment in the office is marked, highlighted, and labeled. Check sheets available for high value equipment. Maintenance is scheduled for critical equipment.		
	XV	Assess the cleanliness of the office.	How dust free are the areas? This may be critical. Look under desks and behind work spaces to see if there is garbage and other unnecessary items.		
	XVI	Assess status of equipment in the area. Cleanliness overall appearance.	Are machines and equipment known to be on a schedule of cleaning?		
			Category Subtotal		
			Shine / Sweep Score: Subtotal divided by 4		
STANDARDIZE	XVII	Is there visual color diagramming and color coding?	A clear and present color coding system is present in the office and across departments. It is clear that standards are being maintained and improved on.		
	XVIII	Assess the access ways in case of emergency.	All emergency systems; fire vehicles, fire extinguishers, and emergency equipment free of obstruction and clear at all times. Access to electrical controls and fuses are known, marked, and free of any obstructions.		
	XIX	The aisle ways are bright with light and clearly marked.	Walkways are clearly highlighted for direction, aisle access identified at any moment.		
	XX	General area has quantity limits for materials and are marked clearly.	Heights are marked, quantity of materials are known, and min vs. max. This includes paper for machines, number of computers required, toner levels, graphical paper, and special office material needed.		
	XXI	Is there clear document control of information in the office?	All information and documentation is controlled, labeled, and revisions are up to date. There are no label-less binders or pieces of paper in the area.		
			Category Subtotal		
			Standardize Score: Subtotal divided by 5		
SUSTAIN	XXII	The aisle ways are clean and maintenance is clear.	Aisles are never full of anything and are clear for passage. All items and products not stored in the aisle and storage is next to aisle accessible for transportation.		
	XXIII	Illustrations and office layout plans are available to compare against.	5S has a maintenance system that allows for control of change and improvement of 5S in the office. Scoring is kept on each of these items and history is present and visible to support future improvement.		
	XXIV	Ability for shared resources and tools to be set back in place for storage.	No self-discipline is necessary to ensure that all stationary, tools, templates, materials, and shared equipment is put back in the same spot. The effort of putting back should not require organizational skills.		
	XXV	Evaluate the involvement of managers in 5S.	Managers are actively involved in the review process of 5S and are supporting improvement activities of the office.		
			Category Subtotal		
			Sustain Score: Subtotal divided by 4		

Total "Category Subtotals" divide by 25 average 5 S score: TOTAL

5S Office Evaluation Review

Date: _____   Evaluation Area: _____

5S Element	Number	Evaluation Criteria	Rank these items from 1 through 5: 5 being well done	Score (1-5)	Ideas / Suggestions / Comments
SORT	I	Are the aisles and walkways open and clear?	All items that are not necessary or unsafe have been removed from the area used as pathways.		
	II	Is the office area free of any spills of fluids?	Consider whether there are any chemicals, water, oils or other materials that may be hazardous in the area or on the floor.		
	III	Is the office area free of unnecessary articles and items?	Are items that are not needed been removed from the work zone, i.e. monitors, scanners, stationary, extra items?		
	IV	Is the office area free of excess consumables/materials?	Evaluate against how many items are in the processing area for work. Assess if the materials, parts, and supplies in the area are currently needed for the job. Closer to actually needed is better.		
	V	Is the information board active?	All announcements are displayed currently and in good presentable shape. Arrangement is straight and placed under appropriate headings.		
	VI	Are the areas walls and dividers free of items not used in the operation?	Extra items are not on the walls, dividers, calendars, or hanging of posters that are not necessary.		
			Category Subtotal		
			Sort Score: Subtotal divided by 6		
SET IN ORDER / STRAIGHTEN	VII	Evaluate any documentation storage.	Only documents required for jobs are stored at the point of use. These documents are stored nicely and in an orderly fashion that is recognizable/understandable to outsiders.		
	VIII	How are the shelves, desks, and work surfaces arranged?	All locations of items are labeled, marked, and it is known if they are missing.		
	IX	How are the tools and materials stored in the area?	No items are resting on walls, tucked in corners. No items are resting on equipment, cupboards, or other fixtures.		
	X	Evaluate container and any packaging locations and tidiness.	Boxes, storage containers, and other items are stored in the appropriate place and orientated well for the area. Cabinets are secure and not causing any danger to the people working in the area.		
	XI	Assess order and where items are found on the floor.	Nothing is sitting directly on the floor and no materials are left around the area. Items that need to be on the floor are clearly marked and positioned in designated areas clearly outlined on the floor.		
	XII	Easiness to access the tools, equipment, and stationary.	Materials, tools, jigs, attachments, and fixtures are organized so that they are all easily within reach. Consider this as well for any kind of tools needed for a job including cutting and measuring something.		
			Category Subtotal		
			Set in Order / Straighten Score: Subtotal divided by 6		
SHINE / SWEEP	XIII	The storage of templates and any tools.	Arrangement of all templates, tools, and materials are kept in clean area for storage and no risk of losing information during movements around office.		
	XIV	Clear when equipment needs maintenance and when last maintained.	Instructions on equipment in the office is marked, highlighted, and labeled. Check sheets available for high value equipment. Maintenance is scheduled for critical equipment.		
	XV	Assess the cleanliness of the office.	How dust free are the areas? This may be critical. Look under desks and behind work spaces to see if there is garbage and other unnecessary items.		
	XVI	Assess status of equipment in the area. Cleanliness overall appearance.	Are machines and equipment known to be on a schedule of cleaning?		
			Category Subtotal		
			Shine / Sweep Score: Subtotal divided by 4		
STANDARDIZE	XVII	Is there visual color diagramming and color coding?	A clear and present color coding system is present in the office and across departments. It is clear that standards are being maintained and improved on.		
	XVIII	Assess the access ways in case of emergency.	All emergency systems; fire vehicles, fire extinguishers, and emergency equipment free of obstruction and clear at all times. Access to electrical controls and fuses are known, marked, and free of any obstructions.		
	XIX	The aisle ways are bright with light and clearly marked.	Walkways are clearly highlighted for direction, aisle access identified at any moment.		
	XX	General area has quantity limits for materials and are marked clearly.	Heights are marked, quantity of materials are known, and min vs. max. This includes paper for machines, number of computers required, toner levels, graphical paper, and special office material needed.		
	XXI	Is there clear document control of information in the office?	All information and documentation is controlled, labeled, and revisions are up to date. There are no label-less binders or pieces of paper in the area.		
			Category Subtotal		
			Standardize Score: Subtotal divided by 5		
SUSTAIN	XXII	The aisle ways are clean and maintenance is clear.	Aisles are never full of anything and are clear for passage. All items and products not stored in the aisle and storage is next to aisle accessible for transportation.		
	XXIII	Illustrations and office layout plans are available to compare against.	5S has a maintenance system that allows for control of change and improvement of 5S in the office. Scoring is kept on each of these items and history is present and visible to support future improvement.		
	XXIV	Ability for shared resources and tools to be set back in place for storage.	No self-discipline is necessary to ensure that all stationary, tools, templates, materials, and shared equipment is put back in the same spot. The effort of putting back should not require organizational skills.		
	XXV	Evaluate the involvement of managers in 5S.	Managers are actively involved in the review process of 5S and are supporting improvement activities of the office.		
			Category Subtotal		
			Sustain Score: Subtotal divided by 4		**Total "Category Subtotals" divide by 25 average 5 S score: TOTAL**

5S Office Evaluation Review

Date: _____   Evaluation Area: _____

5S Element	Number	Evaluation Criteria	Rank these items from 1 through 5: 5 being well done	Score (1-5)	Ideas / Suggestions / Comments
SORT	I	Are the aisles and walkways open and clear?	All items that are not necessary or unsafe have been removed from the area used as pathways.		
	II	Is the office area free of any spills of fluids?	Consider whether there are any chemicals, water, oils or other materials that may be hazardous in the area or on the floor.		
	III	Is the office area free of unnecessary articles and items?	Are items that are not needed been removed from the work zone, i.e. monitors, scanners, stationary, extra items?		
	IV	Is the office area free of excess consumables/materials?	Evaluate against how many items are in the processing area for work. Assess if the materials, parts, and supplies in the area are currently needed for the job. Closer to actually needed is better.		
	V	Is the information board active?	All announcements are displayed currently and in good presentable shape. Arrangement is straight and placed under appropriate headings.		
	VI	Are the areas walls and dividers free of items not used in the operation?	Extra items are not on the walls, dividers, calendars, or hanging of posters that are not necessary.		
			Category Subtotal		
			Sort Score: Subtotal divided by 6		
SET IN ORDER / STRAIGHTEN	VII	Evaluate any documentation storage.	Only documents required for jobs are stored at the point of use. These documents are stored nicely and in an orderly fashion that is recognizable/understandable to outsiders.		
	VIII	How are the shelves, desks, and work surfaces arranged?	All locations of items are labeled, marked, and it is known if they are missing.		
	IX	How are the tools and materials stored in the area?	No items are resting on walls, tucked in corners. No items are resting on equipment, cupboards, or other fixtures.		
	X	Evaluate container and any packaging locations and tidiness.	Boxes, storage containers, and other items are stored in the appropriate place and orientated well for the area. Cabinets are secure and not causing any danger to the people working in the area.		
	XI	Assess order and where items are found on the floor.	Nothing is sitting directly on the floor and no materials are left around the area. Items that need to be on the floor are clearly marked and positioned in designated areas clearly outlined on the floor.		
	XII	Easiness to access the tools, equipment, and stationary.	Materials, tools, jigs, attachments, and fixtures are organized so that they are all easily within reach. Consider this as well for any kind of tools needed for a job including cutting and measuring something.		
			Category Subtotal		
			Set in Order / Straighten Score: Subtotal divided by 6		
SHINE / SWEEP	XIII	The storage of templates and any tools.	Arrangement of all templates, tools, and materials are kept in clean area for storage and no risk of losing information during movements around office.		
	XIV	Clear when equipment needs maintenance and when last maintained.	Instructions on equipment in the office is marked, highlighted, and labeled. Check sheets available for high value equipment. Maintenance is scheduled for critical equipment.		
	XV	Assess the cleanliness of the office.	How dust free are the areas? This may be critical. Look under desks and behind work spaces to see if there is garbage and other unnecessary items.		
	XVI	Assess status of equipment in the area. Cleanliness overall appearance.	Are machines and equipment known to be on a schedule of cleaning?		
			Category Subtotal		
			Shine / Sweep Score: Subtotal divided by 4		
STANDARDIZE	XVII	Is there visual color diagramming and color coding?	A clear and present color coding system is present in the office and across departments. It is clear that standards are being maintained and improved on.		
	XVIII	Assess the access ways in case of emergency.	All emergency systems; fire vehicles, fire extinguishers, and emergency equipment free of obstruction and clear at all times. Access to electrical controls and fuses are known, marked, and free of any obstructions.		
	XIX	The aisle ways are bright with light and clearly marked.	Walkways are clearly highlighted for direction, aisle access identified at any moment.		
	XX	General area has quantity limits for materials and are marked clearly.	Heights are marked, quantity of materials are known, and min vs. max. This includes paper for machines, number of computers required, toner levels, graphical paper, and special office material needed.		
	XXI	Is there clear document control of information in the office?	All information and documentation is controlled, labeled, and revisions are up to date. There are no label-less binders or pieces of paper in the area.		
			Category Subtotal		
			Standardize Score: Subtotal divided by 5		
SUSTAIN	XXII	The aisle ways are clean and maintenance is clear.	Aisles are never full of anything and are clear for passage. All items and products not stored in the aisle and storage is next to aisle accessible for transportation.		
	XXIII	Illustrations and office layout plans are available to compare against.	5S has a maintenance system that allows for control of change and improvement of 5S in the office. Scoring is kept on each of these items and history is present and visible to support future improvement.		
	XXIV	Ability for shared resources and tools to be set back in place for storage.	No self-discipline is necessary to ensure that all stationary, tools, templates, materials, and shared equipment is put back in the same spot. The effort of putting back should not require organizational skills.		
	XXV	Evaluate the involvement of managers in 5S.	Managers are actively involved in the review process of 5S and are supporting improvement activities of the office.		
			Category Subtotal		
			Sustain Score: Subtotal divided by 4		Total "Category Subtotals" divide by 25 average 5 S score: TOTAL

5S Office Evaluation Review

Date: _____   Evaluation Area: _____

5S Element	Number	Evaluation Criteria	Rank these items from 1 through 5: 5 being well done	Score (1-5)	Ideas / Suggestions / Comments
SORT	I	Are the aisles and walkways open and clear?	All items that are not necessary or unsafe have been removed from the area used as pathways.		
	II	Is the office area free of any spills of fluids?	Consider whether there are any chemicals, water, oils or other materials that may be hazardous in the area or on the floor.		
	III	Is the office area free of unnecessary articles and items?	Are items that are not needed been removed from the work zone, i.e. monitors, scanners, stationary, extra items?		
	IV	Is the office area free of excess consumables/materials?	Evaluate against how many items are in the processing area for work. Assess if the materials, parts, and supplies in the area are currently needed for the job. Closer to actually needed is better.		
	V	Is the information board active?	All announcements are displayed currently and in good presentable shape. Arrangement is straight and placed under appropriate headings.		
	VI	Are the areas walls and dividers free of items not used in the operation?	Extra items are not on the walls, dividers, calendars, or hanging of posters that are not necessary.		
			Category Subtotal		
			Sort Score: Subtotal divided by 6		
SET IN ORDER / STRAIGHTEN	VII	Evaluate any documentation storage.	Only documents required for jobs are stored at the point of use. These documents are stored nicely and in an orderly fashion that is recognizable/understandable to outsiders.		
	VIII	How are the shelves, desks, and work surfaces arranged?	All locations of items are labeled, marked, and it is known if they are missing.		
	IX	How are the tools and materials stored in the area?	No items are resting on walls, tucked in corners. No items are resting on equipment, cupboards, or other fixtures.		
	X	Evaluate container and any packaging locations and tidiness.	Boxes, storage containers, and other items are stored in the appropriate place and orientated well for the area. Cabinets are secure and not causing any danger to the people working in the area.		
	XI	Assess order and where items are found on the floor.	Nothing is sitting directly on the floor and no materials are left around the area. Items that need to be on the floor are clearly marked and positioned in designated areas clearly outlined on the floor.		
	XII	Easiness to access the tools, equipment, and stationary.	Materials, tools, jigs, attachments, and fixtures are organized so that they are all easily within reach. Consider this as well for any kind of tools needed for a job including cutting and measuring something.		
			Category Subtotal		
			Set in Order / Straighten Score: Subtotal divided by 6		
SHINE / SWEEP	XIII	The storage of templates and any tools.	Arrangement of all templates, tools, and materials are kept in clean area for storage and no risk of losing information during movements around office.		
	XIV	Clear when equipment needs maintenance and when last maintained.	Instructions on equipment in the office is marked, highlighted, and labeled. Check sheets available for high value equipment. Maintenance is scheduled for critical equipment.		
	XV	Assess the cleanliness of the office.	How dust free are the areas? This may be critical. Look under desks and behind work spaces to see if there is garbage and other unnecessary items.		
	XVI	Assess status of equipment in the area. Cleanliness overall appearance.	Are machines and equipment known to be on a schedule of cleaning?		
			Category Subtotal		
			Shine / Sweep Score: Subtotal divided by 4		
STANDARDIZE	XVII	Is there visual color diagramming and color coding?	A clear and present color coding system is present in the office and across departments. It is clear that standards are being maintained and improved on.		
	XVIII	Assess the access ways in case of emergency.	All emergency systems; fire vehicles, fire extinguishers, and emergency equipment free of obstruction and clear at all times. Access to electrical controls and fuses are known, marked, and free of any obstructions.		
	XIX	The aisle ways are bright with light and clearly marked.	Walkways are clearly highlighted for direction, aisle access identified at any moment.		
	XX	General area has quantity limits for materials and are marked clearly.	Heights are marked, quantity of materials are known, and min vs. max. This includes paper for machines, number of computers required, toner levels, graphical paper, and special office material needed.		
	XXI	Is there clear document control of information in the office?	All information and documentation is controlled, labeled, and revisions are up to date. There are no label-less binders or pieces of paper in the area.		
			Category Subtotal		
			Standardize Score: Subtotal divided by 5		
SUSTAIN	XXII	The aisle ways are clean and maintenance is clear.	Aisles are never full of anything and are clear for passage. All items and products not stored in the aisle and storage is next to aisle accessible for transportation.		
	XXIII	Illustrations and office layout plans are available to compare against.	5S has a maintenance system that allows for control of change and improvement of 5S in the office. Scoring is kept on each of these items and history is present and visible to support future improvement.		
	XXIV	Ability for shared resources and tools to be set back in place for storage.	No self-discipline is necessary to ensure that all stationary, tools, templates, materials, and shared equipment is put back in the same spot. The effort of putting back should not require organizational skills.		
	XXV	Evaluate the involvement of managers in 5S.	Managers are actively involved in the review process of 5S and are supporting improvement activities of the office.		
			Category Subtotal		
			Sustain Score: Subtotal divided by 4		Total "Category Subtotals" divide by 25 average 5 S score: TOTAL

5S Office Evaluation Review

Date: _____   Evaluation Area: _____

5S Element	Number	Evaluation Criteria	Rank these items from 1 through 5: 5 being well done	Score (1-5)	Ideas / Suggestions / Comments
SORT	I	Are the aisles and walkways open and clear?	All items that are not necessary or unsafe have been removed from the area used as pathways.		
	II	Is the office area free of any spills of fluids?	Consider whether there are any chemicals, water, oils or other materials that may be hazardous in the area or on the floor.		
	III	Is the office area free of unnecessary articles and items?	Are items that are not needed been removed from the work zone, i.e. monitors, scanners, stationary, extra items?		
	IV	Is the office area free of excess consumables/materials?	Evaluate against how many items are in the processing area for work. Assess if the materials, parts, and supplies in the area are currently needed for the job. Closer to actually needed is better.		
	V	Is the information board active?	All announcements are displayed currently and in good presentable shape. Arrangement is straight and placed under appropriate headings.		
	VI	Are the areas walls and dividers free of items not used in the operation?	Extra items are not on the walls, dividers, calendars, or hanging of posters that are not necessary.		
			Category Subtotal		
			Sort Score: Subtotal divided by 6		
SET IN ORDER / STRAIGHTEN	VII	Evaluate any documentation storage.	Only documents required for jobs are stored at the point of use. These documents are stored nicely and in an orderly fashion that is recognizable/understandable to outsiders.		
	VIII	How are the shelves, desks, and work surfaces arranged?	All locations of items are labeled, marked, and it is known if they are missing.		
	IX	How are the tools and materials stored in the area?	No items are resting on walls, tucked in corners. No items are resting on equipment, cupboards, or other fixtures.		
	X	Evaluate container and any packaging locations and tidiness.	Boxes, storage containers, and other items are stored in the appropriate place and orientated well for the area. Cabinets are secure and not causing any danger to the people working in the area.		
	XI	Assess order and where items are found on the floor.	Nothing is sitting directly on the floor and no materials are left around the area. Items that need to be on the floor are clearly marked and positioned in designated areas clearly outlined on the floor.		
	XII	Easiness to access the tools, equipment, and stationary.	Materials, tools, jigs, attachments, and fixtures are organized so that they are all easily within reach. Consider this as well for any kind of tools needed for a job including cutting and measuring something.		
			Category Subtotal		
			Set in Order / Straighten Score: Subtotal divided by 6		
SHINE / SWEEP	XIII	The storage of templates and any tools.	Arrangement of all templates, tools, and materials are kept in clean area for storage and no risk of losing information during movements around office.		
	XIV	Clear when equipment needs maintenance and when last maintained.	Instructions on equipment in the office is marked, highlighted, and labeled. Check sheets available for high value equipment. Maintenance is scheduled for critical equipment.		
	XV	Assess the cleanliness of the office.	How dust free are the areas? This may be critical. Look under desks and behind work spaces to see if there is garbage and other unnecessary items.		
	XVI	Assess status of equipment in the area. Cleanliness overall appearance.	Are machines and equipment known to be on a schedule of cleaning?		
			Category Subtotal		
			Shine / Sweep Score: Subtotal divided by 4		
STANDARDIZE	XVII	Is there visual color diagramming and color coding?	A clear and present color coding system is present in the office and across departments. It is clear that standards are being maintained and improved on.		
	XVIII	Assess the access ways in case of emergency.	All emergency systems; fire vehicles, fire extinguishers, and emergency equipment free of obstruction and clear at all times. Access to electrical controls and fuses are known, marked, and free of any obstructions.		
	XIX	The aisle ways are bright with light and clearly marked.	Walkways are clearly highlighted for direction, aisle access identified at any moment.		
	XX	General area has quantity limits for materials and are marked clearly.	Heights are marked, quantity of materials are known, and min vs. max. This includes paper for machines, number of computers required, toner levels, graphical paper, and special office material needed.		
	XXI	Is there clear document control of information in the office?	All information and documentation is controlled, labeled, and revisions are up to date. There are no label-less binders or pieces of paper in the area.		
			Category Subtotal		
			Standardize Score: Subtotal divided by 5		
SUSTAIN	XXII	The aisle ways are clean and maintenance is clear.	Aisles are never full of anything and are clear for passage. All items and products not stored in the aisle and storage is next to aisle accessible for transportation.		
	XXIII	Illustrations and office layout plans are available to compare against.	5S has a maintenance system that allows for control of change and improvement of 5S in the office. Scoring is kept on each of these items and history is present and visible to support future improvement.		
	XXIV	Ability for shared resources and tools to be set back in place for storage.	No self-discipline is necessary to ensure that all stationary, tools, templates, materials, and shared equipment is put back in the same spot. The effort of putting back should not require organizational skills.		
	XXV	Evaluate the involvement of managers in 5S.	Managers are actively involved in the review process of 5S and are supporting improvement activities of the office.		
			Category Subtotal		
			Sustain Score: Subtotal divided by 4		

Total "Category Subtotals" divide by 25 average 5 S score: TOTAL

5S Office Evaluation Review

Date: _____   Evaluation Area: _____

5S Element	Number	Evaluation Criteria	Rank these items from 1 through 5: 5 being well done	Score (1-5)	Ideas / Suggestions / Comments
SORT	I	Are the aisles and walkways open and clear?	All items that are not necessary or unsafe have been removed from the area used as pathways.		
	II	Is the office area free of any spills of fluids?	Consider whether there are any chemicals, water, oils or other materials that may be hazardous in the area or on the floor.		
	III	Is the office area free of unnecessary articles and items?	Are items that are not needed been removed from the work zone, i.e. monitors, scanners, stationary, extra items?		
	IV	Is the office area free of excess consumables/materials?	Evaluate against how many items are in the processing area for work. Assess if the materials, parts, and supplies in the area are currently needed for the job. Closer to actually needed is better.		
	V	Is the information board active?	All announcements are displayed currently and in good presentable shape. Arrangement is straight and placed under appropriate headings.		
	VI	Are the areas walls and dividers free of items not used in the operation?	Extra items are not on the walls, dividers, calendars, or hanging of posters that are not necessary.		
			Category Subtotal		
			Sort Score: Subtotal divided by 6		
SET IN ORDER / STRAIGHTEN	VII	Evaluate any documentation storage.	Only documents required for jobs are stored at the point of use. These documents are stored nicely and in an orderly fashion that is recognizable/understandable to outsiders.		
	VIII	How are the shelves, desks, and work surfaces arranged?	All locations of items are labeled, marked, and it is known if they are missing.		
	IX	How are the tools and materials stored in the area?	No items are resting on walls, tucked in corners. No items are resting on equipment, cupboards, or other fixtures.		
	X	Evaluate container and any packaging locations and tidiness.	Boxes, storage containers, and other items are stored in the appropriate place and orientated well for the area. Cabinets are secure and not causing any danger to the people working in the area.		
	XI	Assess order and where items are found on the floor.	Nothing is sitting directly on the floor and no materials are left around the area. Items that need to be on the floor are clearly marked and positioned in designated areas clearly outlined on the floor.		
	XII	Easiness to access the tools, equipment, and stationary.	Materials, tools, jigs, attachments, and fixtures are organized so that they are all easily within reach. Consider this as well for any kind of tools needed for a job including cutting and measuring something.		
			Category Subtotal		
			Set in Order / Straighten Score: Subtotal divided by 6		
SHINE / SWEEP	XIII	The storage of templates and any tools.	Arrangement of all templates, tools, and materials are kept in clean area for storage and no risk of losing information during movements around office.		
	XIV	Clear when equipment needs maintenance and when last maintained.	Instructions on equipment in the office is marked, highlighted, and labeled. Check sheets available for high value equipment. Maintenance is scheduled for critical equipment.		
	XV	Assess the cleanliness of the office.	How dust free are the areas? This may be critical. Look under desks and behind work spaces to see if there is garbage and other unnecessary items.		
	XVI	Assess status of equipment in the area. Cleanliness overall appearance.	Are machines and equipment known to be on a schedule of cleaning?		
			Category Subtotal		
			Shine / Sweep Score: Subtotal divided by 4		
STANDARDIZE	XVII	Is there visual color diagramming and color coding?	A clear and present color coding system is present in the office and across departments. It is clear that standards are being maintained and improved on.		
	XVIII	Assess the access ways in case of emergency.	All emergency systems; fire vehicles, fire extinguishers, and emergency equipment free of obstruction and clear at all times. Access to electrical controls and fuses are known, marked, and free of any obstructions.		
	XIX	The aisle ways are bright with light and clearly marked.	Walkways are clearly highlighted for direction, aisle access identified at any moment.		
	XX	General area has quantity limits for materials and are marked clearly.	Heights are marked, quantity of materials are known, and min vs. max. This includes paper for machines, number of computers required, toner levels, graphical paper, and special office material needed.		
	XXI	Is there clear document control of information in the office?	All information and documentation is controlled, labeled, and revisions are up to date. There are no label-less binders or pieces of paper in the area.		
			Category Subtotal		
			Standardize Score: Subtotal divided by 5		
SUSTAIN	XXII	The aisle ways are clean and maintenance is clear.	Aisles are never full of anything and are clear for passage. All items and products not stored in the aisle and storage is next to aisle accessible for transportation.		
	XXIII	Illustrations and office layout plans are available to compare against.	5S has a maintenance system that allows for control of change and improvement of 5S in the office. Scoring is kept on each of these items and history is present and visible to support future improvement.		
	XXIV	Ability for shared resources and tools to be set back in place for storage.	No self-discipline is necessary to ensure that all stationary, tools, templates, materials, and shared equipment is put back in the same spot. The effort of putting back should not require organizational skills.		
	XXV	Evaluate the involvement of managers in 5S.	Managers are actively involved in the review process of 5S and are supporting improvement activities of the office.		
			Category Subtotal		
			Sustain Score: Subtotal divided by 4		

Total "Category Subtotals" divide by 25 average 5 S score: TOTAL

5S Office Evaluation Review

Date: _____   Evaluation Area: _____

5S Element	Number	Evaluation Criteria	Rank these items from 1 through 5: 5 being well done	Score (1-5)	Ideas / Suggestions / Comments
SORT	I	Are the aisles and walkways open and clear?	All items that are not necessary or unsafe have been removed from the area used as pathways.		
	II	Is the office area free of any spills of fluids?	Consider whether there are any chemicals, water, oils or other materials that may be hazardous in the area or on the floor.		
	III	Is the office area free of unnecessary articles and items?	Are items that are not needed been removed from the work zone, i.e. monitors, scanners, stationary, extra items?		
	IV	Is the office area free of excess consumables/materials?	Evaluate against how many items are in the processing area for work. Assess if the materials, parts, and supplies in the area are currently needed for the job. Closer to actually needed is better.		
	V	Is the information board active?	All announcements are displayed currently and in good presentable shape. Arrangement is straight and placed under appropriate headings.		
	VI	Are the areas walls and dividers free of items not used in the operation?	Extra items are not on the walls, dividers, calendars, or hanging of posters that are not necessary.		
			Category Subtotal		
			Sort Score: Subtotal divided by 6		
SET IN ORDER / STRAIGHTEN	VII	Evaluate any documentation storage.	Only documents required for jobs are stored at the point of use. These documents are stored nicely and in an orderly fashion that is recognizable/understandable to outsiders.		
	VIII	How are the shelves, desks, and work surfaces arranged?	All locations of items are labeled, marked, and it is known if they are missing.		
	IX	How are the tools and materials stored in the area?	No items are resting on walls, tucked in corners. No items are resting on equipment, cupboards, or other fixtures.		
	X	Evaluate container and any packaging locations and tidiness.	Boxes, storage containers, and other items are stored in the appropriate place and orientated well for the area. Cabinets are secure and not causing any danger to the people working in the area.		
	XI	Assess order and where items are found on the floor.	Nothing is sitting directly on the floor and no materials are left around the area. Items that need to be on the floor are clearly marked and positioned in designated areas clearly outlined on the floor.		
	XII	Easiness to access the tools, equipment, and stationary.	Materials, tools, jigs, attachments, and fixtures are organized so that they are all easily within reach. Consider this as well for any kind of tools needed for a job including cutting and measuring something.		
			Category Subtotal		
			Set in Order / Straighten Score: Subtotal divided by 6		
SHINE / SWEEP	XIII	The storage of templates and any tools.	Arrangement of all templates, tools, and materials are kept in clean area for storage and no risk of losing information during movements around office.		
	XIV	Clear when equipment needs maintenance and when last maintained.	Instructions on equipment in the office is marked, highlighted, and labeled. Check sheets available for high value equipment. Maintenance is scheduled for critical equipment.		
	XV	Assess the cleanliness of the office.	How dust free are the areas? This may be critical. Look under desks and behind work spaces to see if there is garbage and other unnecessary items.		
	XVI	Assess status of equipment in the area. Cleanliness overall appearance.	Are machines and equipment known to be on a schedule of cleaning?		
			Category Subtotal		
			Shine / Sweep Score: Subtotal divided by 4		
STANDARDIZE	XVII	Is there visual color diagramming and color coding?	A clear and present color coding system is present in the office and across departments. It is clear that standards are being maintained and improved on.		
	XVIII	Assess the access ways in case of emergency.	All emergency systems; fire vehicles, fire extinguishers, and emergency equipment free of obstruction and clear at all times. Access to electrical controls and fuses are known, marked, and free of any obstructions.		
	XIX	The aisle ways are bright with light and clearly marked.	Walkways are clearly highlighted for direction, aisle access identified at any moment.		
	XX	General area has quantity limits for materials and are marked clearly.	Heights are marked, quantity of materials are known, and min vs. max. This includes paper for machines, number of computers required, toner levels, graphical paper, and special office material needed.		
	XXI	Is there clear document control of information in the office?	All information and documentation is controlled, labeled, and revisions are up to date. There are no label-less binders or pieces of paper in the area.		
			Category Subtotal		
			Standardize Score: Subtotal divided by 5		
SUSTAIN	XXII	The aisle ways are clean and maintenance is clear.	Aisles are never full of anything and are clear for passage. All items and products not stored in the aisle and storage is next to aisle accessible for transportation.		
	XXIII	Illustrations and office layout plans are available to compare against.	5S has a maintenance system that allows for control of change and improvement of 5S in the office. Scoring is kept on each of these items and history is present and visible to support future improvement.		
	XXIV	Ability for shared resources and tools to be set back in place for storage.	No self-discipline is necessary to ensure that all stationary, tools, templates, materials, and shared equipment is put back in the same spot. The effort of putting back should not require organizational skills.		
	XXV	Evaluate the involvement of managers in 5S.	Managers are actively involved in the review process of 5S and are supporting improvement activities of the office.		
			Category Subtotal		
			Sustain Score: Subtotal divided by 4		Total "Category Subtotals" divide by 25 average 5 S score: TOTAL

5S Office Evaluation Review

Date: _____   Evaluation Area: _____

5S Element	Number	Evaluation Criteria	Rank these items from 1 through 5: 5 being well done	Score (1-5)	Ideas / Suggestions / Comments
SORT	I	Are the aisles and walkways open and clear?	All items that are not necessary or unsafe have been removed from the area used as pathways.		
	II	Is the office area free of any spills of fluids?	Consider whether there are any chemicals, water, oils or other materials that may be hazardous in the area or on the floor.		
	III	Is the office area free of unnecessary articles and items?	Are items that are not needed been removed from the work zone, i.e. monitors, scanners, stationary, extra items?		
	IV	Is the office area free of excess consumables/materials?	Evaluate against how many items are in the processing area for work. Assess if the materials, parts, and supplies in the area are currently needed for the job. Closer to actually needed is better.		
	V	Is the information board active?	All announcements are displayed currently and in good presentable shape. Arrangement is straight and placed under appropriate headings.		
	VI	Are the areas walls and dividers free of items not used in the operation?	Extra items are not on the walls, dividers, calendars, or hanging of posters that are not necessary.		
			Category Subtotal		
			Sort Score: Subtotal divided by 6		
SET IN ORDER / STRAIGHTEN	VII	Evaluate any documentation storage.	Only documents required for jobs are stored at the point of use. These documents are stored nicely and in an orderly fashion that is recognizable/understandable to outsiders.		
	VIII	How are the shelves, desks, and work surfaces arranged?	All locations of items are labeled, marked, and it is known if they are missing.		
	IX	How are the tools and materials stored in the area?	No items are resting on walls, tucked in corners. No items are resting on equipment, cupboards, or other fixtures.		
	X	Evaluate container and any packaging locations and tidiness.	Boxes, storage containers, and other items are stored in the appropriate place and orientated well for the area. Cabinets are secure and not causing any danger to the people working in the area.		
	XI	Assess order and where items are found on the floor.	Nothing is sitting directly on the floor and no materials are left around the area. Items that need to be on the floor are clearly marked and positioned in designated areas clearly outlined on the floor.		
	XII	Easiness to access the tools, equipment, and stationary.	Materials, tools, jigs, attachments, and fixtures are organized so that they are all easily within reach. Consider this as well for any kind of tools needed for a job including cutting and measuring something.		
			Category Subtotal		
			Set in Order / Straighten Score: Subtotal divided by 6		
SHINE / SWEEP	XIII	The storage of templates and any tools.	Arrangement of all templates, tools, and materials are kept in clean area for storage and no risk of losing information during movements around office.		
	XIV	Clear when equipment needs maintenance and when last maintained.	Instructions on equipment in the office is marked, highlighted, and labeled. Check sheets available for high value equipment. Maintenance is scheduled for critical equipment.		
	XV	Assess the cleanliness of the office.	How dust free are the areas? This may be critical. Look under desks and behind work spaces to see if there is garbage and other unnecessary items.		
	XVI	Assess status of equipment in the area. Cleanliness overall appearance.	Are machines and equipment known to be on a schedule of cleaning?		
			Category Subtotal		
			Shine / Sweep Score: Subtotal divided by 4		
STANDARDIZE	XVII	Is there visual color diagramming and color coding?	A clear and present color coding system is present in the office and across departments. It is clear that standards are being maintained and improved on.		
	XVIII	Assess the access ways in case of emergency.	All emergency systems; fire vehicles, fire extinguishers, and emergency equipment free of obstruction and clear at all times. Access to electrical controls and fuses are known, marked, and free of any obstructions.		
	XIX	The aisle ways are bright with light and clearly marked.	Walkways are clearly highlighted for direction, aisle access identified at any moment.		
	XX	General area has quantity limits for materials and are marked clearly.	Heights are marked, quantity of materials are known, and min vs. max. This includes paper for machines, number of computers required, toner levels, graphical paper, and special office material needed.		
	XXI	Is there clear document control of information in the office?	All information and documentation is controlled, labeled, and revisions are up to date. There are no label-less binders or pieces of paper in the area.		
			Category Subtotal		
			Standardize Score: Subtotal divided by 5		
SUSTAIN	XXII	The aisle ways are clean and maintenance is clear.	Aisles are never full of anything and are clear for passage. All items and products not stored in the aisle and storage is next to aisle accessible for transportation.		
	XXIII	Illustrations and office layout plans are available to compare against.	5S has a maintenance system that allows for control of change and improvement of 5S in the office. Scoring is kept on each of these items and history is present and visible to support future improvement.		
	XXIV	Ability for shared resources and tools to be set back in place for storage.	No self-discipline is necessary to ensure that all stationary, tools, templates, materials, and shared equipment is put back in the same spot. The effort of putting back should not require organizational skills.		
	XXV	Evaluate the involvement of managers in 5S.	Managers are actively involved in the review process of 5S and are supporting improvement activities of the office.		
			Category Subtotal		
			Sustain Score: Subtotal divided by 4		**Total "Category Subtotals" divide by 25 average 5 S score: TOTAL**

5S Office Evaluation Review

Date: _____   Evaluation Area: _____

5S Element	Number	Evaluation Criteria	Rank these items from 1 through 5: 5 being well done	Score (1-5)	Ideas / Suggestions / Comments
SORT	I	Are the aisles and walkways open and clear?	All items that are not necessary or unsafe have been removed from the area used as pathways.		
	II	Is the office area free of any spills of fluids?	Consider whether there are any chemicals, water, oils or other materials that may be hazardous in the area or on the floor.		
	III	Is the office area free of unnecessary articles and items?	Are items that are not needed been removed from the work zone, i.e. monitors, scanners, stationary, extra items?		
	IV	Is the office area free of excess consumables/materials?	Evaluate against how many items are in the processing area for work. Assess if the materials, parts, and supplies in the area are currently needed for the job. Closer to actually needed is better.		
	V	Is the information board active?	All announcements are displayed currently and in good presentable shape. Arrangement is straight and placed under appropriate headings.		
	VI	Are the areas walls and dividers free of items not used in the operation?	Extra items are not on the walls, dividers, calendars, or hanging of posters that are not necessary.		
			Category Subtotal		
			Sort Score: Subtotal divided by 6		
SET IN ORDER / STRAIGHTEN	VII	Evaluate any documentation storage.	Only documents required for jobs are stored at the point of use. These documents are stored nicely and in an orderly fashion that is recognizable/understandable to outsiders.		
	VIII	How are the shelves, desks, and work surfaces arranged?	All locations of items are labeled, marked, and it is known if they are missing.		
	IX	How are the tools and materials stored in the area?	No items are resting on walls, tucked in corners. No items are resting on equipment, cupboards, or other fixtures.		
	X	Evaluate container and any packaging locations and tidiness.	Boxes, storage containers, and other items are stored in the appropriate place and orientated well for the area. Cabinets are secure and not causing any danger to the people working in the area.		
	XI	Assess order and where items are found on the floor.	Nothing is sitting directly on the floor and no materials are left around the area. Items that need to be on the floor are clearly marked and positioned in designated areas clearly outlined on the floor.		
	XII	Easiness to access the tools, equipment, and stationary.	Materials, tools, jigs, attachments, and fixtures are organized so that they are all easily within reach. Consider this as well for any kind of tools needed for a job including cutting and measuring something.		
			Category Subtotal		
			Set in Order / Straighten Score: Subtotal divided by 6		
SHINE / SWEEP	XIII	The storage of templates and any tools.	Arrangement of all templates, tools, and materials are kept in clean area for storage and no risk of losing information during movements around office.		
	XIV	Clear when equipment needs maintenance and when last maintained.	Instructions on equipment in the office is marked, highlighted, and labeled. Check sheets available for high value equipment. Maintenance is scheduled for critical equipment.		
	XV	Assess the cleanliness of the office.	How dust free are the areas? This may be critical. Look under desks and behind work spaces to see if there is garbage and other unnecessary items.		
	XVI	Assess status of equipment in the area. Cleanliness overall appearance.	Are machines and equipment known to be on a schedule of cleaning?		
			Category Subtotal		
			Shine / Sweep Score: Subtotal divided by 4		
STANDARDIZE	XVII	Is there visual color diagramming and color coding?	A clear and present color coding system is present in the office and across departments. It is clear that standards are being maintained and improved on.		
	XVIII	Assess the access ways in case of emergency.	All emergency systems; fire vehicles, fire extinguishers, and emergency equipment free of obstruction and clear at all times. Access to electrical controls and fuses are known, marked, and free of any obstructions.		
	XIX	The aisle ways are bright with light and clearly marked.	Walkways are clearly highlighted for direction, aisle access identified at any moment.		
	XX	General area has quantity limits for materials and are marked clearly.	Heights are marked, quantity of materials are known, and min vs. max. This includes paper for machines, number of computers required, toner levels, graphical paper, and special office material needed.		
	XXI	Is there clear document control of information in the office?	All information and documentation is controlled, labeled, and revisions are up to date. There are no label-less binders or pieces of paper in the area.		
			Category Subtotal		
			Standardize Score: Subtotal divided by 5		
SUSTAIN	XXII	The aisle ways are clean and maintenance is clear.	Aisles are never full of anything and are clear for passage. All items and products not stored in the aisle and storage is next to aisle accessible for transportation.		
	XXIII	Illustrations and office layout plans are available to compare against.	5S has a maintenance system that allows for control of change and improvement of 5S in the office. Scoring is kept on each of these items and history is present and visible to support future improvement.		
	XXIV	Ability for shared resources and tools to be set back in place for storage.	No self-discipline is necessary to ensure that all stationary, tools, templates, materials, and shared equipment is put back in the same spot. The effort of putting back should not require organizational skills.		
	XXV	Evaluate the involvement of managers in 5S.	Managers are actively involved in the review process of 5S and are supporting improvement activities of the office.		
			Category Subtotal		
			Sustain Score: Subtotal divided by 4		**Total "Category Subtotals" divide by 25 average 5 S score: TOTAL**